Fifty Hikes
In Vermont

View of Camel's Hump from the Dean Trail

Fifty Hikes in Vermont

Walks, Day Hikes,
and Backpacking Trips
in the Green Mountains

HEATHER AND HUGH SADLIER

Photographs by the authors

THIRD EDITION,
REVISED BY THE GREEN MOUNTAIN CLUB

Backcountry Publications
Woodstock, Vermont

Published by Backcountry Publications, Inc.
Woodstock, Vermont 05091
Printed in the United States of America

Library of Congress Cataloging in Publication Data

Sadlier, Heather.
  Fifty hikes in Vermont.

  Rev. ed. of: Fifty hikes in Vermont / Ruth Sadlier.
Updated 2nd ed. 1981
    1. Hiking—Vermont—Guide-books. 2. Backpacking—
Vermont—Guide-books. 3. Vermont—Description and
travel—1981-   —Guide-books. I. Sadlier, Hugh.
II. Sadlier, Ruth. Fifty hikes in Vermont. III. Green
Mountain Club. IV. Title. V. Title: 50 hikes in
Vermont.
GV199.42.V4S2 1985   917.43′0443   85-8124
ISBN 0-942440-26-9

Photographs on pages 15, 102, and 159 courtesy of the Vermont Development Agency; photograph on page 115 courtesy of Jay Peak, Inc. All other photographs by the authors.

Acknowledgments—The publisher is grateful for the assistance of the Green Mountain Club in the preparation of this edition, especially Preston Bristow, Ray Auger, and Ben Davis. Thanks also to our editor Robin Dutcher-Bayer, and to Duncan Campbell, Bill Guenther, Charles Hine, Bob Lindemann, Jay Maciejowski, Shelly Simpson Mazzola, George F. Pearlstein, Ben Rolston, Winifred Shambo, Al Stiles, Steve Sinclair, John Wiggin, and Philip Woodbury for their contributions.

Cover design by Wladislaw Finne.

Publisher's Note to the Third Edition

When we realized last year that *Fifty Hikes in Vermont* needed revising and discovered that the original authors were not available to do the work, we sought the assistance of the Green Mountain Club. Preston Bristow, President of the GMC, graciously offered the Club's help in the preparation of this third edition. In spite of time constraints, the Green Mountain Club and Backcountry Publications together managed to field check or obtain recent eyewitness accounts of all the 50 hikes in this book in time for spring publication. While Preston acted as Backcountry liaison, Ben Davis and Ray Auger, the Club's Staff Field Assistants, conducted many of the trail checks. Ray's updates of the Stratton Pond and Harmon Hill hikes and Ben's rewriting of the Mt. Mansfield hike are among their valuable contributions. One hike, Pine Hill, was dropped from this edition, and information on its replacement, North Peak Trail, was supplied by Winnie Shambo. Backcountry's in-house editor, Robin Dutcher-Bayer, carefully blended the updates and rewritten passages into the Sadliers' original text, and

her work is deeply appreciated. Also, had it not been for the work of Betsy Bates and Gerald Slager, who were responsible for the previous revision in 1981, considerably greater efforts would have had to be made to bring this edition up to date.

In addition to updating the text, three-quarters of the maps from the second edition were corrected to reflect changes in landmarks and trail locations. Of these, ten were prepared from scratch for this edition.

Future changes in roads, trailheads, property ownership, and the trails themselves will, of course, affect the descriptions in this edition. If you do find the hikes changed from their descriptions here, please let the publisher know so that corrections may be made in future printings. Address comments and suggestions to: Editor, *Fifty Hikes,* Backcountry Publications, P.O. Box 175, Woodstock, VT 05091.

Woodstock, Vermont
May 1985

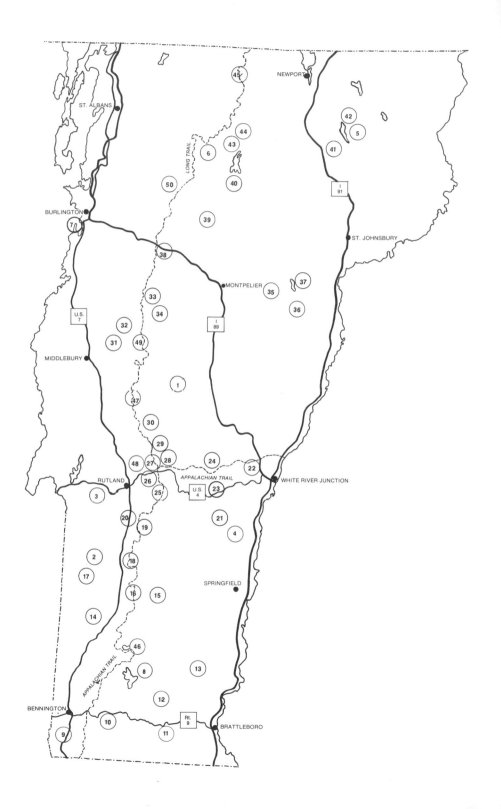

Contents

Introduction

Introductory Hikes

Southern Vermont

Central Vermont

Legend

≡ view
Λ campground
■ shelter
--- main trail
···· side trail
Ⓟ parking
x through trail indicates trail no longer recommended or available

Introduction

With increasing amounts of leisure time, people are turning more to healthy outdoor activities. Hiking and backpacking offer myriad opportunities to gain relief from the complexities and luxuries of our modern world. What we might term the "appeal of the wilds" draws us out into the clean, invigorating air of scenic woodlands and towering mountains. And yet, there is more to hiking than just walking along a trail or looking at a view. We gain appreciation for nature's unique values: simplicity, silence, and solitude. We learn that we must depend more upon ourselves than on external aids. We learn that by "roughing it" we can better appreciate what we have. In the end, we learn more about ourselves.

The Fifty Hikes

We have selected these fifty hikes from all sections of Vermont. Some trips are clearly for experienced hikers only and some are designed for the inexperienced and groups with young children, but the majority will reward any reasonably fit hiker or hiker-to-be. This selection includes trips on Vermont's five highest peaks (all over 4,000 feet) and twenty different excursions of the well-known and well-used Long Trail. The other thirty hikes, however, follow the theme of (Vermont Poet Laureate) Robert Frost's poem "The Road Not Taken." They introduce you to some of the less traveled peaks and areas.

Forty-five of the hikes are day trips (of these, seven are introductory hikes). The remaining five offer chances for extended backpacking journeys. Two can be handled on a normal weekend (two days/one night); two, on a long weekend (three days/two nights); and one, in a week (four days/three nights).

In the four years between publication of the second edition of this guide and the completely revised edition you are now reading, many of the fifty hikes have undergone changes. Some of these alterations in trails or terrain are insignificant, while others are not. This edition was prepared with the advice and help of Green Mountain Club volunteers and GMC's northern and southern staff field assistant. One of the hikes was dropped from this edition, and replaced with the North Peak Trail hike. Six of the hikes were significantly revised to reflect changes in trailhead locations, and to record newly routed sections of existing trails. Three of the backpacking hikes were completely rewritten. In all other cases, changes that had occurred in the years between editions were incorporated into the text of the appropriate hike.

Distance, Hiking Time, Vertical Rise, and Class

These categories appear at the beginning of each hike and give you a summary of what lies ahead. They should help you decide if a particular hike matches your abilities and the time you have available.

Distance gives the mileage, to the nearest tenth, from a hike's start to its finish. Almost all the hikes return you to your starting point, either via a loop or by the same trail. Three of the overnights, Hikes 47, 48, and 49, are exceptions; on these you start at one point and finish miles away, necessitating additional transportation arrangements.

Don't be surprised to find some mileage differences between those listed in this book and the same ones appearing on trail signs erected by the Green Mountain Club and the U.S. Forest Service. For example, we measured the East Branch Trail to Somerset Reservoir at 5.5 miles one way, but read on the Forest Service sign that it was 6.5 miles! We will not try to argue that our distances are the only true ones, although we do believe they are accurate.

Remember that the hiking time means just that; it does not include rest, lunch, or observation stops. Ater a couple of hikes you should know how your pace compares with our steady-but-leisurely one and be able to apply this knowledge to other hikes.

Vertical rise indicates the total amount of *upward* climbing entailed in a hike. Sometimes you will climb up and down valleys before ascending to a summit. Those preliminary upward climbs are included in the vertical rise figure. As a general rule, you can expect that the greater the vertical rise per mile, the more strenuous the hike.

In order to help you determine which hikes are appropriate for you, we have rated each by *class*. The criteria for the classifications are as follows:

Class I: Mostly flat-to-gradual grade; no obstacles.

Class II: Mostly gradual-to-moderate grade with possible isolated steep sections; little, if any, ledge climbing.

Class III: Gradual to mostly moderate grade with occasional steep sections; minimal ledge climbing, possibly requiring use of hands.

Class IV: Moderate-to-steep grade; much ledge climbing; use of hands necessary.

Class V: Mostly steep grade; extensive ledge climbing; much use of hands necessary.

Most people should not be fearful of attempting the hikes in Classes I or II, or even many of those in Class III. If time is not a factor and you can ''go at your own pace'' (which we recommend), you should find all of these within your reach. A few of the hikes in Class III and all those in Classes IV and V are quite

strenuous. These should not be attempted by anyone who does not exercise regularly (active, sinewy youth may be the exception here). Remember that once you are on the trail and beyond the limits of civilization, you must depend upon your feet, legs, back, hands, and cardio-vascular system. Don't attempt more than you can reasonably handle.

Maps

The maps in this edition of the guidebook are based on the United States Geological Survey topographical maps. The hike routes and any important landmarks have been superimposed on the appropriate USGS map or maps for the area. In many cases the maps provided here will be sufficient, but if you are planning to take one of the longer hikes, it would be wise to obtain a separate USGS map to carry with you also. The USGS maps can help orient you should you become lost, and they cover a sufficiently large area so that you can identify more distant peaks when you have clear mountain views.

You should note that only the contours, water bodies, and major roads can be presumed to be accurate on USGS maps. Trails shown on the maps can be dated; a "sideways x" crossing a marked trail on the map indicates an inaccurate or confusing side route, and warns you to stay on the main trail. The USGS maps are usually available at sporting goods stores. They can also be obtained, along with an index to the state of Vermont, directly from the government. Write to: United States Geological Survey, 1200 South Eads Street, Arlington, Virginia 22202.

When hiking on the Long Trail, the Green Mountain Club's *Guide Book of the Long Trail* will be especially helpful. It includes fold-out maps of Camel's Hump and Mount Mansfield. The GMC's *Day Hiker's Guide to Vermont* contains maps and detailed descriptions of over 200 short hikes throughout the state. Information on obtaining these and other GMC publications can be found at the end of this book.

Vermont and the Green Mountains

While touring the lake that now bears his name, on July 4, 1609, Samuel Champlain made the first recorded mention of the Green Mountains. Of all the mountains in the world, they are among the oldest (close to 400 million years old). They once rivaled the heights of such young peaks as Mount McKinley and Mount Rainier.

The bedrock that makes up most of the Green Mountain range was formed beneath the ocean, eons ago, of sea shells, shale, sand, and sedimentary clay. The hot, molten interior of the earth caused great upheavals in the ocean floor, pushing the sea back and giving birth to the mountains—which reared their heads to cool slowly. Fragmentation and additional eruptions in the earth's surface gave rise to other new peaks.

The Ice Age brought glaciers. Organic life was crushed beneath frozen mile-thick masses. During Ice Age "summers," rivers coursed across the face of glaciers and ferried quantities of rocks to southern New England and Long Island Sound. Farmers have been plowing these glacial deposits out of fields and piling them into stone walls for hundreds of years.

The Green Mountains were molded and carved by the thousands of years of glacial advancement and recession. Vermont's mountains today have approximately the same elevation and contours as they did at the time of the final recession of the glaciers.

When only the Indians inhabited America, Vermont was a virtual wilderness. Early settlers appeared and began to cut trees to clear land for cattle, corn, towns, and industries. They also reduced vast numbers of trees to cinders to obtain potash, which was in high demand for English industries. Logging empires of the 1800s ruthlessly slaughtered the virgin forests and exported the lumber to build new towns and cities along the Atlantic coast.

There were continual murmurings from conservationists about the large-scale pillaging of woodlands. In 1891 Joseph Battell confronted the Vermont legislature and pleaded for protection of the wildlands. This "forestry movement" led to the founding of the Forest Association.

In 1912 the duties of this association were extended. State-owned model forests demonstrated the advantages of scientific cutting and planting to private woodlot owners. Forest management for both conservation and commerce came under this single authority. Lumbermen realized that it was good business to replace trees and perhaps increase their numbers, for future harvests.

Other groups have also played roles in preserving some of Vermont's forest lands. Many people were introduced to the Green Mountains at the "Summit Houses." By the 1850s paths had been trodden to most of the highest peaks in Vermont. To accommodate the lucrative city tourist trade, carriage roads were built up most of them. Equinox Mountain, Mount Ascutney, Camel's Hump, Mount Mansfield, Lincoln Mountain, and Snake Mountain all offered bed and board in their summit houses. Sunsets, sunrises, hiking, dancing, and entertainment occupied the guests. Most of the summit houses were eventually lost to declines in business, fires,. . .or porcupines.

The Green Mountain Club has also been instrumental in fostering trail growth and care in Vermont, chiefly along the famous Long Trail, which runs

265 miles from Massachusetts to Canada. The GMC maintains approximately 175 miles of side trails, and more than 70 shelters along the Long Trail. Founded in 1910, the Club has more than 4,000 members (with 14 active sections or chapters), and stations Caretakers at high-use shelters along the Long Trail.

The Caretaker Program dates from the early 1920s when GMC Caretakers were intermittently on duty maintaining the trails and shelters around popular areas on the Long Trail. Today, the Program represents a coordinated effort by the GMC not only to maintain shelters and trails, but also to educate hikers through informal conversation and example. The Caretaker is responsible for the upkeep of his or her shelter, but does not provide services that are normally the hiker's responsibility.

GMC Caretakers are experienced hikers, and are happy to provide backpacking suggestions and tips, as well as basic information on the Green Mountain Club and the Long Trail. They are dedicated to the premise that most hikers, when provided with proper information, will seek to minimize their impact on the trail environment. Ranger-Naturalists are stationed on Camel's Hump and Mount Mansfield; the Long Trail Patrol (founded in 1931), provides basic trail maintenance, and constructs new (and repairs existing) shelters.

The GMC is a tremendous resource for hikers, and can be contacted for the most current information on trail changes. Call or write for updates, and information on GMC activities, publications, and membership: The Green Mountain Club, 43 State Street, Box 889 Montpelier, VT 05602 (802-223-3463).

Seasonal Hiking

The Vermont hiking season is limited only by your preference and ability. Fall is one of our favorite times to go. When the leaves start to turn, you are treated to one of nature's wonders. Cool air and rainbow colors combine to give you a "natural high." Few regions of the world possess the large tracts of broadleaved trees and favorable weather conditions that produce the vivid fall colors we enjoy in Vermont. As the air gets crisper and leaves tumble, light snow blankets the trails. Not deep enough to be a hindrance, this covering is dotted with animal tracks that unfold like a story book as you walk along.

Spring brings sprouting greens and lingering reminders of winter, but hiking at higher elevations on the Long Trail, and anywhere in the state, is officially discouraged in the early spring. The reason for this is that hiker's boots can damage wet and muddy trails. Hikers are asked to exercise good judgement in assessing the condition of a particular trail—lingering snow at higher elevations is the best sign of wet trails. Both Camel's Hump and Mount Mansfield are closed to hikers during mud season, and open on Memorial Day weekend.

June and July offer plenty of sunny days—and bugs. Take along plenty of insect repellent. If you like the feel of sweat dropping off your brow and dampening the small of your back, July and August are the months for you. September sees the end of bugs, but the days are still warm and the skies are often crystal clear.

Rules and Regulations

You do not leave these behind when departing from civilization. Most rules and regulations have been developed to help us preserve woodlands and the wildlife living therein. Philosophies such as "leave nothing but footprints" carry important messages, but they are not specific enough to check the careless rush of mankind.

Rangers patrolling Mount Mansfield

Fire regulations in Vermont can vary, depending on whether you build a fire on state, federal, or privately-owned land (contact the GMC for information on specific hikes). The GMC encourages the use of portable backpacking stoves, rather than open fires.

Fees are collected for use of state park facilities and some Long Trail shelters.

Groups should limit their size to 10 (four to six is the ideal size), and take tents or tarps when planning overnights in case shelters are crowded. At certain high-use shelters on state land (such as Mount Mansfield), *no* camping is permitted near the shelter. Groups should avoid these areas on weekends.

Hikers who take dogs along with them

should note that Vermont's state parks have leash laws. In general, hikers are encouraged to leave their pets at home.

For additional information about hiking on Federal lands, contact: Forest Supervisor, Green Mountain National Forest, Rutland, Vermont 05701. Further information about hiking on state forest lands or in state parks can be obtained from: Department of Forest, Parks, and Recreation, Agency of Environmental Conservation, Montpelier, Vermont 05602.

First Aid and Safety

The best medicine is prevention. Become familiar with what lies ahead, bring suitable supplies, and know what to do in an emergency.

Traveling alone can be the greatest potential danger to hikers. *Do not underestimate this danger.* With no one to assist in case of accident the chances of serious complications are great.

Brush up on first-aid procedures and bring a first-aid kit with you. Have a compass and map and know how to use them. In Vermont the compass points about 15 degrees west of true north. Take a flashlight and extra batteries, just in case. If you do become lost or injured, don't panic. Remain calm, assess your situation, and act according to your knowledge of the area.

Whether you plan a day hike or a backpacking trip, you should carry some foodstuffs beyond what you expect to consume, at least enough for one extra meal. For an energy treat, you might consider cheese rather than chocolate. Cheeses have a high energy output; the drier ones, such as Romano, Parmesan, Provolone, and Kasseri, are the best. Even relatively dry Swiss and Cheddar have a high water content, so weigh more. Most people do not realize that because of its high fat content (more than fifty percent in unsweetened

varieties), chocolate is much harder to digest than other candy. Eating large amounts of it just before or during strenuous activity often produces an upset stomach, instead of a spurt of energy.

Be sure you wear clothing that is appropriate to your planned hike, and then pack some extra garments. If you are climbing a mountain you will need long pants because of unpredictable temperature changes at higher elevations. Wide-legged, light-weight rainpants are both warm and dry, and they pull on easily over boots. Cotton chamois shirts provide good button-over warmth. You should always carry a woolen sweater. Wool, even if it gets wet, will keep you warm. And the hooded parka of a rainsuit can serve as either wetgear or windbreaker. We bring along featherweight rainsuits on even the sunniest of days.

Preserving Our Heritage

Finally, here are some guidelines for insuring that what we enjoy today will be there for others to enjoy tomorrow:

• Keep your group small; less than six is best.
• Stay only one or two days in one place.
• Leave campsites cleaner than you found them.
• Carry out empty what you carried in full.
• Pick up the litter of less thoughtful persons.
• Wash away from the water supply, not in it.
• Bury body wastes in a shallow hole far from surface water.
• Carry a portable stove for cooking.
• Do not cut trees or branches.
• Protect the delicate ecosystems of the higher elevations.
• Leave no sign of your presence.

1

Texas Falls Nature Trail

Class: I
Distance (round trip): 1.2 miles
Hiking time: 3/4 hour
USGS 7.5' Bread Loaf

The 293,000-acre Green Mountain National Forest offers a wide variety of natural attractions. This showcase of preserved land stretches nearly two-thirds the length of Vermont. A trip through the forest is not just a hike in the woods but rather an excursion into Vermont itself. Rolling countryside, small towns, and slackening pace typify the simpler, quieter way of life that is Vermont.

A leisurely walk through the Texas Falls Recreation Area, on the eastern edge of the Green Mountain National Forest near Hancock, will introduce you to the state's natural endowments. Here the Hancock Branch of the White River pours its waters through an awesome descending gorge in a unique display of nature's magnitude. Twenty-four explanatory guideposts along the nature trail help you better understand the forest's ways and the need for its careful management in today's technological world.

On the Robert Frost Memorial Drive (VT 125), go east 12.9 miles from Middlebury or west 3 miles from Hancock. Turn north onto the road for the Texas Falls National Forest Recreation Area. After .5 mile you will reach a parking area on the left and a sign for the Texas Falls observation site on the right.

A path leads from the road down some stone steps to an attractive setting. A combination wood and stone fence guides you along the trail. You see below a deep gorge with water rushing through. Flowing from a flat pool up to the left, it gushes down into a white, frothy basin. Then slithering over a smooth ledge, it winds and spills its way to quieter pools below. Towering hemlocks help focus your view upon the surging water.

Wind your way up more manmade stone steps to the signed intersection where you will find a box containing the brochure which describes the marked stops along the trail. Bear left at this brochure box.

Almost immediately you come to post #3. The dying and decaying trees of the forest help to enrich the soil around them with new organic material. Leaves and other natural materials fall to the ground and decay, adding more vital nutrients to the soil. At this station you will observe logs undergoing the process of decay.

The flat, spongy trail leads on to post

#4. The source of the Hancock Branch is a forested watershed. Because of the overhanging branches and foliage of the trees and the carpet of leaves on the forest floor protecting the soil from rain erosion, the stream remains unmuddied.

Post #7 marks the location of a massive boulder. Through the process of symbiosis, a plant community thrives on top of this great rock. Its greenish-grey, crustlike growth is a type of lichen and is composed of two distinctly different plants. Water is collected by the sponge-like fungus. The alga uses this water in photosynthesis to produce food for both itself and the fungus. Thus, these two plants are mutually interdependent; neither could live alone on the rock's surface.

As you continue along the path, you will begin a slight ascent. The river will branch off to the left, crossing beneath the road at a bridge near guidepost #9. You will notice yellow birch and other trees forming a canopy above you.

Just after a bend in the trail you reach post #13. The rows of small holes girdling this Eastern Hemlock were made by a yellow-bellied sapsucker. This woodpecker digs out holes and eats the inner

Texas Falls

bark. During this process sap oozes from the wound. The sapsucker returns later to feast upon any insects attracted to the sap.

The trail now bears to the right, just before you reach the paved road. On the other side of the road is a large picnic area with tables overlooking the river. You may want to stop here for lunch before continuing on the upper loop of the trail. (The next section, is .75 mile, about a 45-minute walk.)

An old logging road leads you along this upper loop of the Nature Trail. About midway, you will come to station #17, which marks the entrance to a deer yard, where groups of white-tailed deer collect in winter. Soon you will notice Eastern Hemlocks around you. The large Hemlock at station #18 has a hole in its base which is the entrance to a chipmunk's burrow.

Hemlocks may grow to eighty feet in height and three feet in diameter. They feature irregularly arranged, half-inch-long needles with twin silvery lines on the underside. Unlike balsam, hemlock needles are not fragrant when crushed. The hemlock is part of the diet of a variety of wild-life. Porcupines chew on the bark, and the seeds are eaten by squirrels and birds.

Look for large, rectangular holes in the tree at station #20. These distinctive marks show that Vermont's largest woodpecker, the Pileated Woodpecker, has been drilling for food in these woods. These birds are extremely shy, but impossible to miss should you be lucky enough to spot one at work—look for its spectacularly brilliant scarlet head.

Near station #23, you will see low growing plants known as Hobblebush. or witch hobble. They are a favorite food of deer. Look closely to see if any of their tops have been nibbled.

Just after station #24, a spur trail to your left will lead you to an overlook below the gorge you saw at the beginning of the trail. The sound of pounding water fills your ears as you look the length of the gorge and see several waterfalls, one atop the other.

Return to the trail intersection, and look for the Brochure box. You can return the Nature Trail guide here, and retrace your steps to the road and parking area.

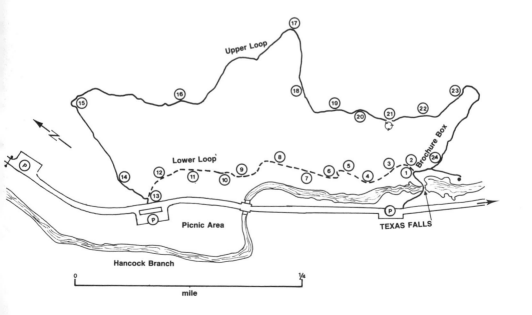

Merck Forest Nature Trail

Class: I
Distance (round trip): 1 mile
Hiking time: 1 hour
Vertical rise: 400 feet
USGS 7.5' Pawlet

The 2,600 acres of woodland, meadows, ponds, and streams that comprise the Merck Forest in Rupert were set aside by George W. Merck in 1950. He felt a close kinship to the land and believed that these fields and forests represented typical Vermont upland farms, then rapidly dying out as commercial ventures. He foresaw that rapidly increasing numbers of outdoor enthusiasts would buy up and otherwise dominate Vermont's open lands and realized the need to preserve extensive areas for public use. He also hoped that the Merck Forest could show how farms might be converted to multiple-use properties.

The Merck Forest, which is run by a private foundation, is made up of several abandoned farms. Although much of the original grazing land has become forest (through both natural seeding and planting), some of the meadows are mowed to keep a balance between forest and open land. A year-round program of logging and reforestation maintains the forest's productivity. The wildlife habitats that result provide suitable homes for a variety of animals. The forest also helps visitors become better acquainted with,

and more understanding of, their environment.

This hike can be enjoyed by the entire family. Its relatively short length allows for leisurely walking and plenty of exploration.

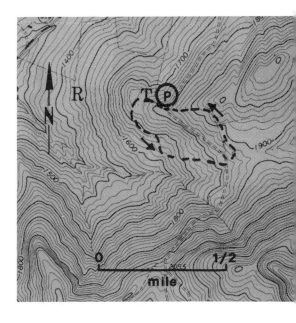

You reach the entrance to the Merck Forest on VT 315 by driving 3.3 miles east from the junction of VT 315 and VT 153 in Rupert, or 2.6 miles west from the junction of VT 315 and VT 30 in East Rupert. Turn south onto the Merck Forest Road, which immediately forks. Bear right and drive .5 mile to the parking area. Walk to the information area near the gate. Register (for Merck Forest rules, see Hike 17) and pick up the pamphlet which describes the ten stations along The Discovery Trail. The trail leads down a gradual slope, along a flat area bordering on a field, and then back up a hill. Take the time to stop at each station and read the corresponding information in the pamphlet. You'll learn about soil and climatic conditions, control of animal populations, and forest life cycles.

This first loop of the hike ends after .5 mile, near the barn which is the center of the Merck Forest education program. Here you will find exhibits which in-troduce you to the many plants and animals that appear in the forest. Instruction in conservation education, as well as other helpful information is provided by the qualified staff.

Before leaving the barn, pick up a pamphlet for the Tree Identification Trail which you will follow on the last section of this hike. You pass by the garden, and the pasture for the pigs near the barn, and walk a route marked with numbered trees which are identified and described in the trail pamphlet. One of the nicest parts of this hike is the Spruce Loop. The trees are so thick here that the outside world is completely cut off. Stop awhile at the bench and enjoy the solitude of the dense forest.

After walking .5 mile, you will find yourself back at the parking lot where you began. Be sure to return the trail pamphlets at the end of your walk so they may be used by others.

Merck Forest Nature Trail

North Peak Trail (Birdseye Hiking Trail)

Class: II
Distance (round trip): 3.4 miles
Hiking time: 3 hours
Vertical rise: 1230 feet
USGS 7 1/2' West Rutland

This hike takes you on the North Peak Trail, one of a series of trails which link the four summits of the Birdseye Mountain Recreational Area. These hiking trails were established in 1979 as a service project by camps Betsey Cox, Killoleet, Keewaydin, and Sangamon. Three trails (North Peak, Castle Peak, and the Butterfly Loop) interconnect on the summit ridge offering opportunities for trips of varying lengths.

To reach the North Peak Trail, follow VT 4A 2.6 miles west of West Rutland. Turn left off of Route 4A and cross over the Castleton River. You will see the base lodge of an abandoned ski area, and can park your car here. As you walk past the lodge you pass the large cement poles which once supported the ski area's chair lift. Go right at the second of these poles, and follow a dirt road through the pine trees until you come to a sharp left in the road (.1 mile). A log may cross the path here, but continue straight and look for the orange-red blazes of the North Peak Trail. The trail itself is not well maintained and may be somewhat overgrown in late summer, but it is well marked with flagging and blazes.

You ascend through an old clearing, and soon enter pine woods. At .2 mile, you cross a telephone and power line clearing, and then the trail leads into mixed hardwoods. Recent logging activity has left the trail littered with debris here, and you may have to scramble around the rotting remains of treetops left crossing the trail. Look for a small footbridge which crosses a normally dry brook bed at .3 mile. From here the trail ascends on easy grades until it reaches a well-defined road at .5 mile, which it follows around a shoulder of the mountain. Fir trees surround the trail here.

Soon, the road turns to the left and levels out, but the trail bears right. You now climb through open woods, crossing a road at .9 mile, and again at 1 mile. Follow the orange-red blazes here onto yet another road which ascends steadily at moderately steep grades. You cross one more well-used road before the trail begins a short steep climb to Killoleet Rock (1.3 miles). Here you can rest while looking through a "tunnel" which has been cut into the trees, providing a lookout to the west.

The trail continues and turns sharply to the left, beginning a slabbing climb up

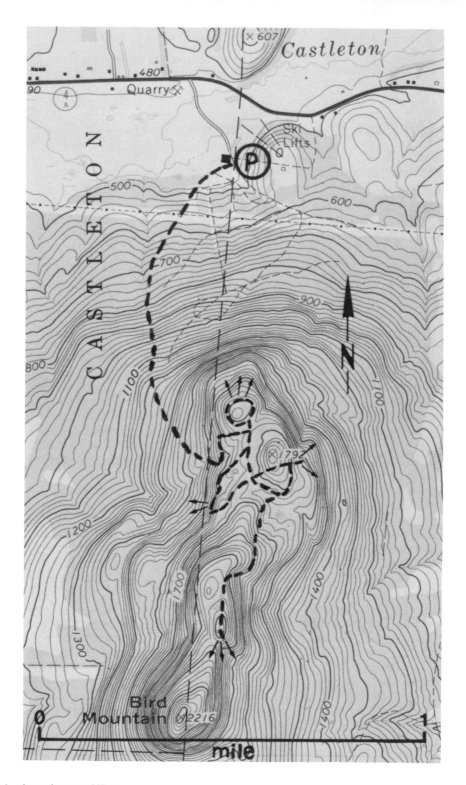

the mountain. At 1.4 miles, the trail crosses an overgrown road, and continues on easier grades to Keewaydin Ledge (1.5 miles), where you can enjoy more extensive views to the west. The trail now bears to the right and ascends gradually. At 1.6 miles you come to North Peak Junction, where the Butterfly and Castle Peak Trails turn off to the right. The North Peak Trail continues straight ahead and quickly reaches the beginning of a loop which circles the summit of North Peak. A short spur trail to the right leads to East Birdseye Lookout, where you see the Castleton River valley stretched out below. You also look out over the communities of West Rutland, Proctor, and Rutland.

Retrace your steps to the main trail and pass over the highest point on North Peak to another spur which leads to the right. From North Birdseye Lookout you can see Grandpa Knob, and the Adirondacks. The main trail continues on from here to a third spur which leads to West Birdseye Lookout (1.7 miles).

The trail soon completes the summit loop, turns to the right, and you retrace your path to North Peak Junction (1.8 miles). If you have time, you may want to follow the signs for the trail to Castle Peak, which continues .8 mile south along the summit ridge.

Return to your car at the base lodge following the same route.

The Pinnacle

Class: II
Distance (round trip): 1 mile
Hiking time: 1/2 hour
Vertical rise: 300 feet
USGS 15' Claremont, NH–VT

A check of old maps indicated that the Pinnacle was formerly called Plum Hill—after the Plum family who lived nearby. Its modern name, however, is a bit misleading. It is little more than a big hill.

The Pinnacle rises alongside the winding Connecticut River in Weathersfield. The Connecticut used to be a prime source of drinking water for domesticated animals. Although cows come to mind first when we think of Vermont farm animals, sheep were the state's principal livestock in the 1830s. William Jarvis, the American consul in Lisbon, imported the first Merino (long-haired) sheep to the United States in 1811 and bred them for forty-eight years on his farm in nearby Weathersfield Bow. This brought about significant changes in the woolen industry and stimulated the growth of sheep raising in the East.

Families will find the climb up the Pinnacle a pleasant outing. A wide, gradual path leads lazily upward. With its elevation of 610 feet, the peak doesn't promise you wide, far-reaching views. But the open overlook nestled in the summit's snowy white birches directs your gaze down the peaceful Connecticut River Valley to the rolling hills of New Hampshire.

The Pinnacle is a part of Wilgus State Park. From the junction of VT 131 and US 5 (and Interstate 91 exit 8) in Ascutney village, drive south on US 5 for 1.1 miles to the park entrance on the left. Check in with the Park Ranger before leaving your car at the picnic area parking lot. (The park also has tent and trailer sites.) Cross US 5 and walk to the trail's start just north of the park entrance. Dogs should be kept on a leash.

This blue-blazed trail begins gradually and quickly makes a switchback upward to the left. Paralleling the road below, you follow a wide, flat trail between stands of hardwoods. In the fall you may identify these trees by the leaves and fruit they shed on the ground. The oval, blunt-based leaves of the birches turn yellow. The coarse-toothed, egg-shaped leaves of the beech are light brown and often veined with yellow. Long, lobed leaves—usually light brown—and familiar acorns announce the presence of oaks. White pines spill five-clustered needles.

After this long, gradual stretch of walking, you start a swing to the right. The hillside drops off steeply to the left. Hemlocks appear frequently along the trail. Their shorter, irregularly arranged

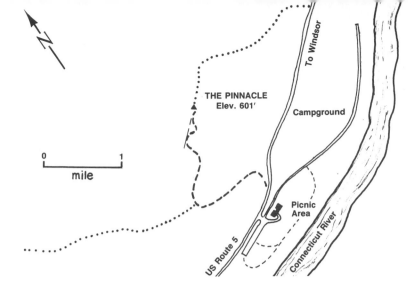

THE PINNACLE
Elev. 601'

To Windsor

Campground

Picnic Area

Connecticut River

US Route 5

N

0   1
└─────────┘
    mile

needles help distinguish them from the balsam fir. Tiny cones and rough bark further identify these evergreens.

Stands of slender white birches predominate as the path bears right. These tall, striking trees are accented by the soft green of intermingling white pine. At approximately .2 mile, the wider trail you have been following bears left, and a narrower route bears right. Take the latter route, which soon crosses a recently-used logging road and becomes an ascending trail.

Birds abound. Watch for the hermit thrush—the Vermont State Bird. This songbird can adapt to a variety of habitats. It may live in swamps or dry uplands, overgrown pastures or thick woodlands. Though the hermit thrush exhibits a marked preference for coniferous forests, it will also abide in predominately deciduous ones. This brown bird's white breast is speckled with flecks of brown. Its bell-like song is especially pretty. The call is a low cluck-

ing, followed by a mewing sound. When disturbed, it shows its displeasure by slowly raising its tail.

You will now begin the final ascent, on the steepest section of the trail, with well-placed stone steps easing the steep pitch as you continue to climb. The trail traverses the slope from right to left, then turns right and heads straight for the summit.

After cresting two small slopes, you turn right. From here it is a short walk to the small partial clearing ringed by white birches that is the top of the Pinnacle. There is ample room to stretch out and enjoy the pastoral setting that unfolds to the east. You have a view through the trees of the Connecticut River and the New Hampshire hills.

Although the blazed trail does continue steeply down to a point on US 5 .3 miles north of the park entrance, it is more pleasant to retrace your steps to the starting point.

Mount Hor

Class: II
Distance (round trip): 3.1 miles
Hiking time: 2 hours
Vertical rise: 748 feet
USGS 15' Lyndonville

The Mount Hor Trail, in Willoughby State Forest (see Hike 41), is a good one for leisurely leg stretching and relaxed enjoyment of panoramic views. The climb is gradual, making it an ideal trip for families and beginning hikers. The views from the overlooks at and near the summit of Mount Hor will appeal to everyone.

Much of the land in this forest has been logged out quite recently, so there is an absence of mature trees. Following common practice, the state of Vermont purchased the land after it was logged for a reasonable price. This wise method of procuring large tracts has made a beautIfully primitive area available to the public.

The Mount Hor Trail is one of many trails in Willoughby State Forest maintained by the Trail Committee of the Westmore Association. This group provides a valuable and much needed service—asking, in return, only that hikers cooperate by not spreading litter along the trails. Why not carry a small bag with you and collect whatever rubbish you come upon?

To reach the gravel access road to Mount Hor, follow VT 5A for 5.7 miles from the junction of VT 5A and US 5 in West Burke or an equal distance from the intersection of VT 5A and VT 16 in Westmore. Watch for a sign to the Pisgah Mountain Trail opposite the access road. Turn in here and follow the gravel road through the woods for 1.8 miles. The Mount Hor parking area is on the right. After leaving your car, walk south along the road approximately 150 feet to the start of the trail, on the right.

The way begins as a rocky path that leads gradually upward through dense side growth. Blackberry bushes edge the trail. If you happen by in the late summer, their tangy sweetness is yours for the picking

The trail rises briefly and then flattens out. Its sides are densely covered with young maples, elms, and birches, and with goldenrod. It is difficult to see beyond the edges of the trail because of the closely packed trees. Winding slowly upward to the right, the path levels out again. The trail is marked by dark blue blazes, with occasional black-arrowed white signs lending assistance. The going gets rockier as you near the top.

Would you normally cancel a hike because of inclement weather? If so, we ask you to reconsider if rain threatens to spoil your plans for this one—Mount Hor is a very walkable rainy day hike. Hiking in the rain produces a world of new experiences if you are properly attired. While it is necessary to pick your way more gingerly, the compensations are worth the effort. Rain beating on your body makes you feel more a part of the outdoor experience. There is also a grey-green softness to the woods during rain that is absent when the sun is shining brightly.

The trail begins an upward swing to the left over bare logs laid latticelike across the path. They provide firm footing across the soft black mud beneath. Although the way climbs relentlessly uphill now, it is rock-free and quite easy going.

The trail climbs straight and more steeply. Notice the sassafras growing to the right. It is most easily identified by its forward-pointing three-lobed leaf. Clusters of dark blue berries ripen in September. Sassafras tea was a product of colonial times, and oil of sassafras was once used widely as a medicine. It is still used to perfume soap.

At the .7-mile mark the trail reaches a junction. White signs guide you left to the summit (West Lookout) and right to Willoughby Lookout. Follow the trail to the left .2 mile to the summit.

This winding spur route is marked by pale blue blazes. You have to step around or over many trees and stumps.

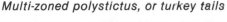
Multi-zoned polystictus, or turkey tails

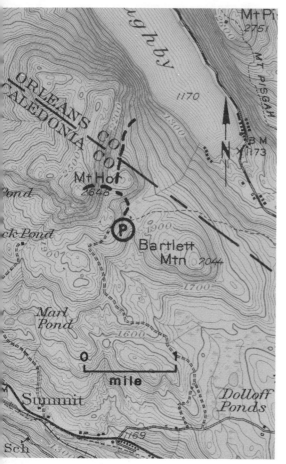

Shortly the path passes over a small streamlet. Continue on this rough route as it winds upward and dips into a clearing. From here the view is to the west, encompassing ten small ponds in the valley below. They sparkle among the heavily wooded areas of Willoughby State Forest. In the distant background portions of the Green Mountains are also visible.

Return to the junction and follow the trail to Willoughby Lookout, .6 mile away. The blazes here are dark blue, and the trail is mostly flat. The way turns sharply right past a lone white birch and a small hemlock and then rises slightly. It levels out and passes a small gulch on the left. The path is soft and spongy as you pass downed trees festooned with turkey tail fungus.

The trail climbs a slight incline and then forks. Swing right and down a short embankment. A breath-taking vista—Mount Pisgah towering above the southern end of Lake Willoughby—unfolds before you. On a clear day you can catch sight of some of the White Mountains in the distance.

Return to the trail junction and follow your original route back to the access road.

Prospect Rock

Class: II
Distance (round trip): 1.5 miles
Hiking time: 1 hour
Vertical rise: 530 feet
USGS 15' Hyde Park

This hike curls pleasantly through cool woods, then climbs upward for the last invigorating quarter-mile to Prospect Rock. It's a satisfying trip for everyone. Experienced hikers should not omit this one because of its brevity or small vertical rise. The rock's 1,050-foot vantage point offers a prime view of the Lamoille River Valley with Sterling Range as a backdrop. You can also survey the northern slope of Mount Mansfield to the south.

Prospect Rock is on the Long Trail. This section of the trail is maintained by the Sterling Section of the Green Mountain Club. To reach the access to the trail, drive west on VT 15 from the junction of VT 100C and VT 15 in Johnson. After 1.8 miles, bear right onto the Johnson-Waterville Road. This turn is just before the Lamoille River bridge. Drive .9 mile on this road to the Ithiel Falls Camp Meeting Ground on the left. Directly across the road the Long Trail leads north up the hill and into the woods. There is very limited parking along the side of the road in front of the campground. More parking is available at an off-the-road area .2 mile east.

The Ithiel Falls Camp Meeting Ground has been in existence for over seventy-five years. Each summer the Nazarene Church sponsors a nondenominational

gathering of people from across the country at this lovely location. Camping here is available only to church members.

Follow the white blazes of the Long Trail up a gravel road and bear left into the woods on an abandoned logging road. A brown and white sign indicates that you are on the Long Trail North heading for Prospect Rock. On entering the woods you cross a quick-flowing

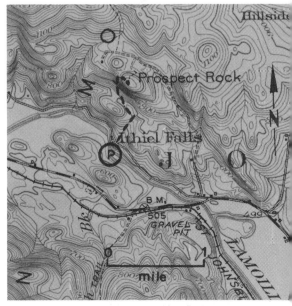

View from Prospect Rock to Whiteface Mountain

brook. Don't be surprised to see the trail cross it two more times.

This first part of the hike is along a rather broad, gradual path through the woods. Abundant greenery edges the way. Look for the hay-scented fern. Common at lower elevations, it also grows in alpine forests. It thrives in moist, partially shaded areas. The dry fronds exude the fragrant odor of hay.

Logs offer footing through occasional soft, black, muddy areas. You make your way up the narrow, gently inclined trail. Numbers of young red spruce crowd the path.

The trail dips into the subdued light of an older stand of spruce. Footsteps are muffled by spruce spills over the soft earth. Sun glows softly through the thick web of branches and past the limbless reddish-brown trunks. Ahead, the trail begins a sudden, steep climb through open woods. A rugged hiking stick will serve you well here. When you reach the top of this slope, bear to your right. Mushrooms and shining club moss border the trail.

Very soon you'll walk out onto Prospect Rock. Although there is no sign to mark this ledge, you will readily recognize it by the views of the Sterling Range and the Lamoille River Valley that stretch before you.

Return via the same route.

7

Red Rocks Park

Class: I
Distance (around loops): 2 1/2 miles
Hiking time: 1 3/4 hours
Vertical rise: 182 feet
USGS 7.5' Burlington

If you are looking for someplace that combines peaceful woods, dramatic cliffs, outstanding lake and mountain views, and a narrow sandy beach, then make your way to Red Rocks Park. Located on the shores of Lake Champlain and Shelburne Bay, the one-hundred-acre park was purchased by the City of South Burlington in 1970 from the Hatch family, who had owned the land since 1895. Red Rocks is one of the few public accesses to Lake Champlain in Vermont. Its more than 2½ miles of interconnected trails are maintained by the South Burlington Recreation Department and are suitable for hikers and strollers of all ages. The area is also well used by cross-country skiers in winter.

To reach the park from I-89, take I-189 (exit 13) to the Shelburne-US 7 South exit, which will have you heading toward Shelburne on US 7. After only a few hundred feet, bear right onto Queen City Park Road. Stay on this road for .4 mile; after crossing a one-lane bridge, look for Central Avenue, the first road on the left. The main entrance to Red Rocks is on your right .1 mile. At the ticket house here you can pick up a free brochure with a trail map and information on the park. The city charges a small fee from late June to early fall for parking in the main lot, but other times of the year you may simply leave your car along Central Avenue just before the main entrance drive.

To explore the park's interior first, saving the grand sweep of the panoramas along the lake cliffs for the end of your hike, start on the trails at either the northeast or northwest corner of the summer parking lot. Bearing right at major intersections, you'll wind slowly through the dense woods. On this leg you will also reach the park's highest point, 282 feet above sea level and about 200 feet higher than Lake Champlain. The view from here extends in all directions, encompassing the Green Mountains to the east, the city of Burlington to the north, and the Adirondacks to the west. Mount Mansfield is clearly visible some twenty-two miles away.

In about 1.5 winding miles, you will reach the overlook at the park's western end, where Shelburne Bay meets Lake Champlain. Shelburne Point is just across the bay's mouth; the island to its right is Juniper Island. Rock Dunder is approximately midway between Shelburne Point and Juniper Island.

Now begin working your way back, staying parallel to the mile-long shoreline of Shelburne Bay. Numerous other overlooks provide equally spectacular views of the Green Mountain and the Adirondacks. There is no access to the lake from this trail, however. The cliffs drop abruptly ninety feet to the water's edge.

Most people will want to conclude their hike with a short walk from the parking lot to the narrow, 800-foot-long sandy beach at the park's southeast corner—and perhaps a swim. There are also picnic tables and rest rooms adjacent to the beach.

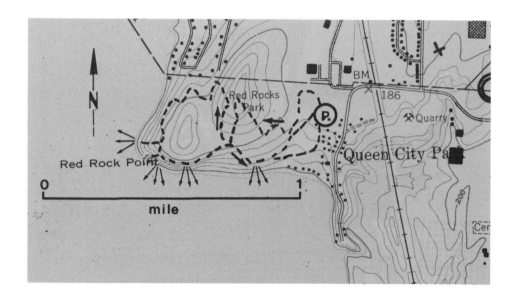

Southern Vermont

Somerset Reservoir

Class: II
Distance (round trip): 10.8 miles
Hiking time: 5 1/2 hours
Vertical rise: 475 feet
USGS 15' Wilmington

If you want a full day of hiking, try the East Branch Trail to Somerset Reservoir. The route has you crossing two different rivers, skirting beaver dams, and meandering undemandingly through a number of naturally varied areas. With the prospect of a picnic at the reservoir, this hike has all the ingredients for a very satisfying day. Do note the distance and hiking time, though. You will want to allow plenty of time for rest and observation stops and for that picnic lunch. Don't get caught short or you may be forced to complete your hike in darkness.

The East Branch Trail was originally put in by the Civilian Conservation Corps as a fire trail. Formerly maintained by the U.S. Forest Service, the route is now maintained by the New England Power Company (NEPCO), which owns most of the property traversed by the trail. The trail is presently marked with clearly defined, double, yellow blazes, except for a section that runs through U.S. Forest Service Land. Nearly all the trail is on Power Company property, and hikers are reminded that overnight camping and open fires are prohibited.

To reach the start of the East Branch Trail from the intersection of VT 9 and VT 100 in Wilmington, go west on Route 9 for 5.4 miles. Here turn right onto a dirt road—a few yards in you'll see a sign for "Picnic Area—NEPCO"—and drive 2 miles to the trailhead. Limited parking is available at the trailhead. Park along the widened side of the road. If you look down the path, you will see a sign for the Deerfield River.

Descending from the road, the trail crosses the West Branch of the Deerfield River on a suspension bridge and proceeds gradually uphill to the north. Approximately 250 feet from the suspension bridge, the East Branch Trail turns sharply uphill to the right. The Flood Dam Trail, also maintained by the New England Power Company, appears on the left, running in a northerly direction. Evergreens mix with deciduous trees as the route leads you gently up and down to the next bridge, at .4 mile, crossing the East Branch of the Deerfield River.

The trail reaches an old railroad bed, where it turns to the north following the grade. Along this bed are several scenic overlooks of the river as well as views of Mount Snow to the northeast. The trail crosses seven streams, some of which can be easily crossed at fords or on hewn timbers that span the stream channel. A good sense of balance can be helpful.

After crossing the last brook, the trail bears to the right, leaving the railroad bed. Soon the trail crosses another brook on a hewn timber, then begins down a slight grade, and returns to the railroad bed. The trail then crosses two more streams, bears to the right of a third stream off the main railroad bed, and follows a spur railroad bed running up the stream, quickly bearing away from the river. As it swings away from the river, the trail passes through a concentrated area of low spruces.

After crossing the stream, the trail crosses into the Green Mountain National Forest (U.S. Forest Service), marked by a red-blazed boundary at 2.9 miles. At the present time, the double, yellow trail blazes end here. Hikers should look for old blue blazes or more recently placed yellow or pink flagging.

The trail follows the brook channel, crosses the brook at 3.0 miles, and at the first fork in the brook bears right (east). At the second fork the trail bears left. Look carefully for trail markings since the trail is somewhat difficult to follow in this area.

The trail begins to level off and crosses the brook for the last time, proceeding in a northwest direction over a level bench of hardwoods. Descending across a red boundary line, the trail crosses back into New England Power Company land at 4.1 miles, where the trail is once again identified by double, yellow paint blazes. You'll be able to see Mount Snow and several beaver ponds here. Hundreds of barkless, sun-bleached logs lie strewn across the land. A deserted beaver

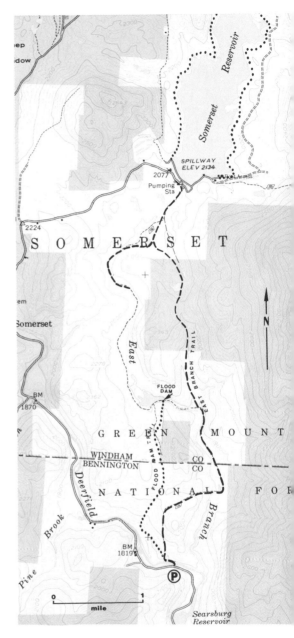

lodge can now be reached via dry land. It provides a good close-up of a beaver home.

After beavers have created a pond,

Beaver lodge

muskrats often move in to enjoy it. Mink, which love muskrat meat, are the next to arrive. Although the beavers have moved on, mink still live here. You may see their droppings on the East Branch Trail.

The trail continues to descend gradually alongside a small stream into a large clearing. You will see the East Branch Spur Trail off to your left, leading to the East Branch of the Deerfield River. The main East Branch Trail turns sharply to the right at this junction and follows the upper edge of a small meadow.

After returning to the woods, the trail once again reaches the East Branch River at 4.7 miles, following the river's east bank for several hundred feet, and then turning away again to the right. Climbing up a moderate grade, the trail levels off and passes to the right of an old mill foundation. The trail then ascends to the right and reaches its terminus on the Somerset Reservoir access road just below the east end of the dam.

From the trail junction, the access road continues a few hundred feet uphill to the top of the dam to parking and boat launching areas. There is a picnic grove at the south end of the East Shore Trail.

The picnic area is also the jumping off point for several other hikes around Somerset Reservoir. To the left of the East Branch Trail junction, the access road descends a short distance to the dam's outlet.

Filling the horizon at the far end of Somerset Reservoir is Stratton Mountain. Glastonbury Mountain rises to the west and, by walking to the left a bit, you can see Mount Snow to the east.

The Dome

Class: III
Distance (round trip): 4.6 miles
Hiking time: 2 1/2 hours
Vertical rise: 1,648 feet
USGS 7.5' Pownal; USGS 7.5' Williamstown, MA

A tangy treat awaits you about three-quarters of the way up this trail: wild raspberries stand ready to delight your tastebuds and add a special bonus to this hike. A gradual-to-moderate climb, this hike has you scrambling over ledge as you near the Dome's summit. Once there, you'll see how this mountain got its name: a massive bulk of rounded ledge swells upward out of the surrounding terrain.

From the junction of US 7 and VT 346 in Pownal, drive south on US 7 for 2.6 miles and turn left onto Sand Springs Road. Follow it, bearing right as the road forks, for .6 mile. Go left onto White Oaks Road. Drive 1.4 miles, past the Broad Brook Trail, past the dead-end sign, to an old road leading into the woods on the right. This is the start of the Dome Trail, which is maintained by the Williams Outing Club. Park off the road here.

Blazes for the Dome Trail are orange painted over white—resulting in a creamy color (a few of the white blazes, though, have not been painted over and some are still bright orange). There are numerous side trails on this hike which could lure the unwary hiker off the path. Be sure to follow the blazes. As the trail progresses, these become less distinct, but by looking carefully, you can follow them the entire way.

After leading briefly through woods, the old road becomes grassy and passes through an open field. It crosses between lines of aspen and leads through a second field. Re-entering the woods, it becomes both level and smooth. The way proceeds gradually upward. Large-toothed aspen and birches dominate the woods with their respective greenish-yellow and white trunks.

Climbing a moderate grade to the left, the road becomes rutted and rocky. Walking is easiest along the left side. You turn sharply left after cresting this grade and pass along the ridge top.

After .5 mile you come to a three-way fork. Follow the Dome Trail to the left. It makes a quick swing back to the right and continues over rocks and roots. At times the trail gouges into the earth as it struggles upward.

Another fork appears at .7 mile. Look closely and you'll see that the two paths rejoin up ahead. Follow either one. Large rocks fill the trail as it winds up through young woods. Countless thin trees swarm around occasional older, thick ones.

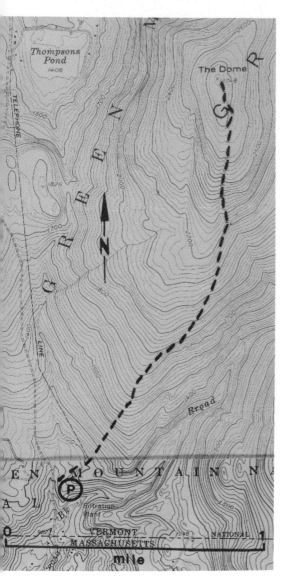

Scattered pines edge the trail as it climbs gradually below a ridge line. These are red pines, identifiable by their three-to-eight-inch needles in cluster of twos. The bark plates have a reddish tinge and the needles lift upward on branch ends.

At 1.4 miles the trail intersects another old road. The remains of a junked truck mark this spot and indicate that, in the not-too-distant past, these slopes were the site of much more activity than is apparent from their present virgin appearance. Turn right and follow the road through a section of woods clogged by numerous downed trees.

At 1.5 miles you will come to a fork. Turn right and ascend a moderate slope (look for the dim marker). Cresting a short, steep slope, you see masses of ledge above to the right. The path loops around behind the ledge and begins a short, steep climb. Dead beech trees support hundreds of multi-zoned polystictus. These pore fungi have thin leathery fans marked by dull-colored, concentric bands. Because of their beautiful markings, they have been nicknamed "turkey tails".

The light grey smoothness of beeches fills the woods on both sides of the trail. Various-sized rocks in the path make walking a bit adventurous. The gradual-to-moderate incline continues.

An old grassy trail branches right at 1.8 miles. Go straight ahead here. Cross several small brooks and climb along the edge of a slope as the hillside rises steeply above.

The path jogs sharply left and passes many raspberry bushes. The arching, reddish branches have prickly thorns. White flowers appear from May through July, and the red fruit ripens from June through October. There are also delicious blackberries here in early September. You'll be returning by the same route, so if you plan much berry-

The Agawon Trail branches off to the right at 1 mile. Continue straight here. A sign on a big boulder marks the Dome Trail. Note the numerous oak trees throughout this area. The acorns from these trees provide food for songbirds, grouse, mourning dove, deer, bear, fox, raccoon, squirrels, and chipmunks.

The summit of the Dome

picking it can wait until then.

As you climb higher, the trail twists and turns through evergreens. Spruce and balsam thicken the woods from ground level to towering heights.

The path winds around and over pieces of ledge. You step up onto a small cone of ledge surrounded by evergreens—and may think this is the top. It's not. Climb down the other side and follow the blazes up onto open ledge, amidst more spruce and balsam.

The summit lies atop a large section of smooth, humpy, white ledge lined with orange-brown streaks. Trees surround this area and block views to the north. The Adirondacks are to the northwest, the Taconics are to the west, and Mount Greylock in Williamstown, Massachusetts is to the south.

10

Harmon Hill

Class: III
Distance (round trip): 3.4 miles
Hiking time: 2 hours
Vertical rise: 965 feet
USGS 7.5' Bennington; USGS 7.5' Pownal;
USGS 7.5' Woodford; USGS 7.5' Stamford

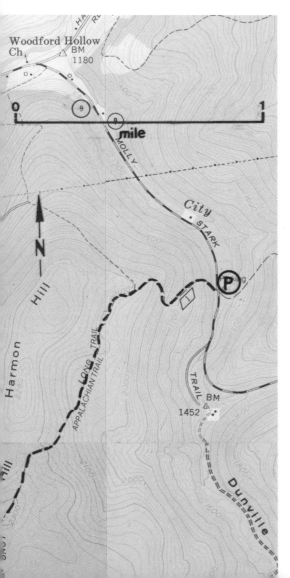

It is best to do some limbering up before this particular climb. Otherwise, the steep beginning of the short hike on the Long Trail will leave you surprised and breathless.

The open, grassy summit of Harmon Hill allows good views to the north and west from its southwestern-corner-of-the-state vantage point. It also invites you to spread a cloth for a picnic lunch or to stretch out on your back for cloud watching. Red raspberries abound here in late July and early August.

From the junction of VT 9 and US 7 in Bennington, drive east 5.2 miles on VT 9 to the well-signed Long Trail crossing. On your left is a large paved parking area; park here and not at the state pull over area on the right (south) side of VT 9. Coming from the east, look for the Long Trail crossing 4.8 miles west of Woodford State Park.

To begin your hike, cross VT 9 to the wooden Long Trail sign in the above mentioned state pull over area. The Long Trail (white blazes) crosses a small log footbridge and begins an extremely steep climb utilizing log and rock steps. These steps were not placed to make your walk easier, but were built by trail maintainers as an erosion control device.

View from Harmon Hill to Bennington; Mount Anthony beyond

Runoff water is slowed by the steps, preventing gullies, until diverted off the trail by log waterbars. You can help keep the trail from eroding by not walking around these structures, thus creating new routes for water to follow.

After .6 mile the trail bears left and soon levels off, passing through a stand of spruce trees. Hardwood trees are making inroads, and in time this area will be an entirely hardwood forest. At your feet are bracken ferns. Commonest of Vermont's ferns, bracken is one of the earliest to appear and continues producing new leaves all season. It grows in large colonies and in poor soils where only the rankest weeds will grow, unlike most ferns which grow in rich, moist, limy areas. Killed by first frost, Bracken wilts fast, often producing sizable areas of crisp brown erect growth.

Leaving the spruce and bracken, the trail soon begins rising through new growth hardwoods and thick shrubs, emerging at 1.5 miles into the open. Ravens have been spotted in this area. They are larger than the common crow, with a wing span reaching to four feet. They frequently glide in flight, wings fully extended. At home along the seacoasts as well as inland, these omnivorous birds have adopted a favorite seagull trick. They will break open shellfish by dropping them onto rocks from high above.

Meandering through fields of tall grass, you walk out onto rounded ledge at 1.7 miles. A signpost officially marks this spot as Harmon Hill (2,325 feet).

High elevation clearings such as this are rare in the Green Mountain National Forest. To maintain the opening for recreation and wildlife, this area is periodically burned by the U.S. Forest Service. Songbirds abound here: note the bluebird boxes scattered throughout the clearing. Many species of wildlife, such as deer and bear, depend on these openings for their forage. Without burning, hardwoods would soon take over the area. Burning also maintains the excellent vista.

Mount Anthony (2,340 feet) rises above Bennington, which spreads below to the west. The city's historic battle monument towers pointedly from its center. Glastenbury Mountain is the 3,748-foot giant to the northeast. Almost due north, and closer, is Bald Mountain. Trees rim the other exposures of the summit and obstruct views in those directions.

Your return is by the same route. Be sure and stop by Stamford Stream on the north side of VT 9 to soak your tired feet.

11

Mount Olga

Class: II
Distance (round trip): 1.5 miles
Hiking time: 1 hour
Vertical rise: 515 feet
USGS 15' Wilmington

The hiking trail to Mount Olga begins in Molly Stark State Park in Wilmington. Molly Stark gave vital and historic aid to her husband, General John Stark, during the Battle of Bennington in 1777. In the first week of August of that year she received an urgent missive from the General:

"Dear Molly: In less than a week, the British forces will be ours. Send every man from the farm that will come and let the haying go."

In addition to the men from their own farm, Molly rounded up two hundred others to join General Stark in battle. For her reward, she received one of the six brass cannons the triumphant Americans captured from the British during the battle.* (The Molly Stark Cannon is now displayed in the New Boston, New Hampshire, town library.)

The mountain you climb on this hike is also named for a woman of generous spirit. Olga Haslund deeded the peak to the State of Vermont with the understanding that it would be called after her.

*From a brochure on Molly State Park; Vermont Department of Forests and Parks.

To reach Molly Stark State Park, drive east on VT 9 (The Molly Stark Trail) for 3.4 miles from the junction of VT 9 and VT 100 in Wilmington. There is a green state park sign at the entrance. Make your way to the administration building to pay the modest facilities fee, then follow the sign to the parking area. If you are taking any dogs with you on this hike, the park asks that you have them on a leash not more than seven feet long. You should also note that this park closes during the first week in October.

Follow the grassy road that starts to the left front of the administration building and travels south to a small clearing and a trail junction. Here bear left, following the sign for Mount Olga. (The white-blazed Ghost Trail to the right leads to the park's camping and picnic area and has been specifically designed as a short and easy hike.)

Follow the blue markers .2 mile to another trail junction. Here a sign points left to "fire tower." Go left onto the blue-blazed trail, which leads to the fire tower on Mount Olga's summit. (The way right is the Stone Wall Trail, which also runs to the park's camping and picnic area.)

A representative inhabitant of this

area is the distinctively plumed barred owl. Its head, neck, and upper breast feathers form dark bars across a lighter colored background. Since this owl's small feet are not large enough to capture sizable prey, its diet consists mainly of mice—which it catches in open country near its home deep in the woods.

Try answering the barred owl's call (four evenly pitched hoots, then the same repeated), or make a squeaking sound with your mouth against the back of your hand. One of these large, inquisitive birds may appear in a nearby tree at any time of day to inspect you carefully with its dark brown eyes.

The wider blue-blazed trail leads upward more steeply. Occasionally you have to scramble around rocks or small boulders. On either side of the path are open deciduous forests dominated by beech trees.

After slabbing the slope to the left, the way levels out and passes between two giant sections of ledge. Becoming narrower, the path passes red blazes on the right at .6 mile. These mark the boundary line of Molly Stark State Park.

The path frequently twists and turns through short evergreens as it approaches the top of Mount Olga. Just below the summit a blue-blazed trail joins from the left. This will be your return route. Go right to an old road and turn right again. Follow this road to the top (2,415 feet).

Transmitting antennae, three small buildings, and a fire tower crowd the small, open summit. From the tower you can scan the surrounding countryside in all directions. Three peaks are particularly prominent. Hogback Mountain (2,410 feet) is in the near northeast. To the northwest is 3,425-foot Haystack Mountain, and 3,556-foot Mount Snow is to the north-northwest.

Follow the path back down the old road and left to the junction of the two blue-blazed trails. Go right here. Your descent, though moderately steep at times, is cushioned by the evergreen spills that thickly cover the path. The trail sides are filled with spruce and balsam fir.

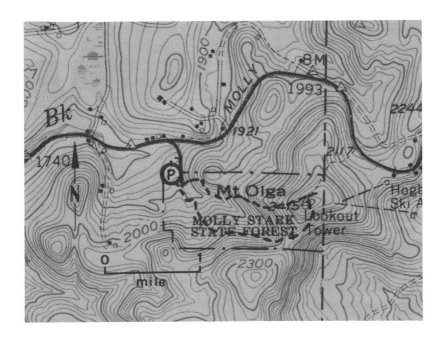

Along the trail to Mount Olga

At 1.1 miles the way leads through a stone wall. This is still a quietly pretty trail. The sound of your steps is muffled by the needles covering the path. The light filters softly through thick branches.

At 1.2 miles this trail intersects an unused footpath that joins from the left. Go right here and continue down the slope. In contrast to the deciduous woods you passed through on the way up, the return route has meandered down through a seemingly endless evergreen forest. Small, bushy "youngsters" are scattered amongst the taller, slimmer parent trees. There are also a few thick-trunked "grandparent" spruces.

At 1.4 miles you cut through another stone wall. Soon you cross a wooden-planked bridge over a small brook. The trail then steps up to the park road just across from the administration building.

12

Haystack Mountain

Class: III
Distance (round trip): 4.8 miles
Hiking time: 3 hours
Vertical rise: 1,242 feet
USGS 15' Wilmington

Prepare for a picnic — and a sun-soaking — on the summit of Haystack Mountain. A brief but rugged ascent takes you to its small, evergreen-enclosed peak.

You begin using your "path finding" skills early as you search for the start of the Haystack Mountain Trail. Some years back there was a fairly direct route from VT 9 north to the trail. However, the spread of civilization in general and the rise of a community of new houses and roads in particular make finding the trailhead a bit more challenging today.

From the junction of VT 100 and VT 9 in Wilmington, drive west on VT 9. After 1.1 miles, turn north onto Haystack Road at the Chimney Hill sign. Follow this road for 1.2 miles to another Chimney Hill sign. Turn left here onto Chimney Hill Road.

Take the next right onto Binney Brook Road. Follow its turning, angling route past Howe's Loop, Large Maple Way, Lila Lane, and the upper end of Howe's Loop. At the T intersection with Twin Chimney Road go right and continue to the next T intersection. Go left onto Upper Dam Road. Drive past Rocky Split Way and another (unnamed) paved road. Just beyond it, on the right, the Haystack Mountain Trail begins as a dirt road, leading away from Upper Dam Road at a

30-degree angle. Park along the edge of the wider section of the paved road.

A remarkably friendly group of chickadees may herald your arrival. Whistle their chick-a-dee notes, and they may venture closer for a noisy inspection. You may see both the black-capped and the smaller, brown-capped species, although the brown-capped chickadees favor higher elevations. Both species prefer to nest in natural cavities or old woodpecker holes in rotten stumps. They feed primarily on insects.

The old dirt road climbs moderately from Upper Dam Road. Although somewhat rutted and rocky, it is smooth enough to let you set a rhythmic pace. At about .1 mile another old road joins from the right. Continue straight and make your way around or under the car chain across the road.

There are no blazes to direct you along the occasionally boggy road. However, the way is well cleared, and the narrower trail that ascends to the summit is a well-beaten one. The vertical rise along the road is consistently gradual. At .4 mile turn left and follow orange blazes while ascending the ridge west of Haystack Mountain. This is a recent relocation of the Haystack Mountain Trail, cut to accommodate snow-

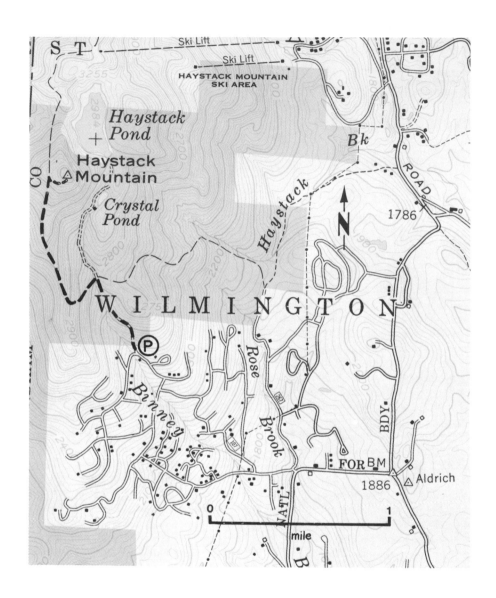

mobile and norpine ski traffic in the winter. It is well marked with orange blazes.

You're likely to see animal droppings atop the small boulders in and around the trail. Weasels are one animal noted for depositing their scats on these rocks.

Also, they tend to use the same spot again and again, so there may be both old and new accumulations. There will be pieces of fur and bone in their slender two-inch droppings.

At 2.0 miles you reach a blue-blazed spur, which leads to the summit. The snowmobile trail continues to Haystack ski area. Nearing the summit, you pass through an area fragrant with evergreens and glistening with birches. Shortly before reaching the top, the needle-covered trail levels out and bears sharply right.

You emerge onto the summit at 2.4 miles. The small, ledged area nestles within a circle of evergreens. Rocks warmed by the sun invite you to stretch out and warm yourself too. Climb up onto the highest piece of ledge to examine the views. Over and between the trees you can see 3,556-foot Mount Pisgah (Mount Snow) to the north. Wide, bare swaths of ski trails scar its slopes. The lofty blue shape on the northeast horizon is Mount Ascutney. Directly below, to the northeast, is Haystack Pond. This is the water supply for the town of Wilmington.

Far to the east you can see New Hampshire's 3,165-foot Monadnock Mountain. To the south is Harriman Reservoir. In the distant southeast is 3,491-foot Mount Greylock, the highest point in Massachusetts. Much of the view to the west and north is blocked by trees.

When you are ready to return, follow the same route by which you ascended.

13

Bald Mountain (Townshend State Forest)

Class: III
Distance (round trip): 3.1 miles
Hiking time: 4 hours
Vertical rise: 1,140 feet
USGS 15' Saxtons River

"Bald" is by far the most popular name for Vermont's treeless peaks. Whatever the reason for such popularity, Vermont's "Bald Mountains" must be further identified by their geographical locations. This hike takes you to the summit of 1,680-foot Bald Mountain in the Townshend State Forest in the southeastern quarter of the state.

The short, steep climb to this peak will challenge those in above-average physical condition. The trail rises 1,140 feet in only 1.1 miles.

On VT 30 drive 2.5 miles south from the steepled white church in West Townshend or 2 miles north from the junction of VT 30 and VT 35 in Townshend. Go west onto the narrow steel bridge at the Townshend Dam. This impressive structure was built between 1959 and 1961 by the U.S. Army Corps of Engineers to control flood waters in the Connecticut River Basin. It is operated for the protection of downstream areas in Vermont, New Hampshire, Massachusetts, and Connecticut. During the record storms of June 30-July 4, 1973, it held back millions of gallons of water, thereby preventing possible loss of life and heavy damage in downstream communities.

Follow the road over the bridge and dam to its end and go left. Just before turning sharply right the road approaches the Scott Covered Bridge. Built in 1870, this is the longest single span (165.7 feet) of its type in Vermont.

Continuing on the same road you will shortly see the main entrance to the Townshend State Forest Camping Area (1.7 miles from the dam). Turn in here, and park in the lot that appears on your right as you approach the main building. Stop in at the office and pay your 75¢ per-person, per-day use fee and ask for the state forest pamphlet for the hiking trail to Bald Mountain. Note that no pets are allowed in this state forest, and that it is officially open only from Memorial Day to Columbus Day.

To reach your starting point, take the road that went to your left when you first pulled into the State Park. After a short walk through the campground, you will find the trailhead at the end of the campground loop near campsite #6.

At the beginning of the trail, notice the huge towering evergreen on your right. This is an eastern white pine tree, the most valuable tree species in Vermont. A few trees of this size would provide enough lumber to build the average sized home. The trail immediately starts to rise, somewhat steeply at first, then levels out at about .2 mile. During this first stretch, the majestic white pines are growing with a varied group of hardwoods including beech, sugar and red maples, and somewhat surprisingly, black birch. This is about the farthest north that black birch grows near the Connecticut River valley. Black birch, or sweet birch, as some people call it, can be identified by its black bark that is smooth on young trees, blotchy on older trees, and its aromatic smell when the twigs are broken. Oil of wintergreen may be extracted from the twigs and bark of sweet birch.

Continuing steeply up the trail again, you will soon see a patch of dense evergreens at about .5 mile. These conifers are mostly eastern hemlock trees, a species which is rapidly becoming an important timber species. The hemlock has another very important use, though. With its thick, dense crown it provides excellent cover in the winter months for white tailed deer. So little snow is able to penetrate the thick canopy that the deer are able to move about with much less restriction. This area is designated a deer wintering area by the State Fish & Wildlife Department.

The trail levels off at .8 mile as it approaches another group of hardwoods. In summer, when the leaves are out, not much of a view is obtained; but during the leafless season, a good vista exists looking north across the West River Valley. At 1.0 mile, the trail climbs upward in a steep ascent across the north face of Bald Mountain. You approach another stand of the dense crowned hemlock. Notice how blocky the bark appears on these trees. This is a sign of very slow growth due to a lack of deep soil and poor environmental conditions. The path now contours the hillside through the hemlock and turns sharply left at 1.2 miles.

The last .2 mile to the top is a little less steep, but climbs over ledge and large boulders. Near the top of this climb you

View of Scott Covered Bridge and Bald Mountain

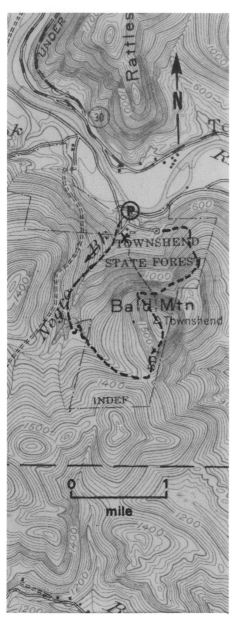

will see small, ground-level caves dotting the hillside. Formed by rocks piled together, they provide ideal homes for porcupines. As the top is approached, look for a large evergreen (white pine) on your right. Notice how the branches seem to have been removed on the western side of the tree. This strange appearance, called krummholz, is caused by very strong prevailing winds, that literally blow the foliage off one side of the tree.

The flat summit is composed of ledge and grass. To the right is an open vista looking northwest. Stratton Mountain dominates the left side of this view. Return to the trail and follow the sign to the south vista. Actually looking southeast, you peer down into the valley of the West River. Across a high ridge line are tiny distant peaks. New Hampshire mountains poke their heads up on the left horizon.

Follow the blue blazes down the more gentle south side of the mountain. The path steepens somewhat and then flattens out. White pine needles cushion the way.

Approximately .3 mile from the summit the trail passes an alder swamp behind you and off the trail on the left. These trees, which are closely related to the birches, have white cross marks on their brown bark. In the eastern United States they are shrub or small tree size. The leaves have short stems and strong, slanted veins. Beavers use alders for both food and building materials.

Swinging to the southwest, the trail continues to descend to a right turn at 1.9 miles. The old trail used to go straight here, but it has been relocated to a more scenic route near the brook. After making this turn, the new trail passes several small cascades along the brook, crosses the brook and goes past an old cellar hole, and joins the remnants of an old logging road. The trail next passes through a hemlock forest, then through a short patch of hardwoods and into a hemlock forest once again. The path makes several switchbacks, crosses a recently used logging road, and rejoins the old trail at 2.5 miles.

Bearing right, the trail begins its descent to the valley below, soon reaching Negro Brook. The brook is crossed on rocks and then the trail starts to follow an old woods road steadily downhill.

Don't be surprised if you see trees with exceptionally large leaves through this area. The basswood linden has eight-inch leaves that are sharply-toothed and unequally heart-shaped at the base. This is a tree with many by-products. Its soft wood is used for excelsior and lumber. American Indians made rope from the rough inner bark and medicinal tea from the fruit. The flowers are a good source of honey.

The trail continues its descent beside the brook. At 3.0 miles the trail crosses the brook again, this time on a wooden bridge, makes a jog to the left, and then immediately turns right to a paved road at campsite #29. Turn right and follow this road uphill, past the park head-quarters, and back to the parking lot.

14

Mount Equinox

Class: IV
Distance (round trip): 6 miles
Hiking time: 4 hours
Vertical rise: 2,861 feet
USGS 7.5' Manchester

Many legends have been handed down about this mountain's name. A popular but fictitious one centered around Captain Partridge, one-time director of the American Literary and Scientific Academy. During the autumnal equinox on September 19, 1832, the captain marched a group of cadets to the summit, where they conducted barometric measurements. Most probably, Equinox derives from the Indian word "Ewanok" meaning "the-place-where-the-top-is."

Mount Equinox is the highest mountain in Vermont not on or adjacent to the Long Trail. At more than 3,800 feet it is also the highest peak overlooking the Vermont Valley, which extends from Bennington to Rutland.

Because of malaria in the lowlands and the Indians' fear of high mountains, nineteenth-century settlers populated the slopes of Equinox. During those times the mountain teemed with trails. Lack of interest and need, however, have allowed them to become overgrown. Today the Burr and Burton Trail ascends directly from the valley to the summit. (Two others connect the Sky Line Drive Toll Road with Lookout Rock.)

The climb up the Burr and Burton Trail begins gradually but soon becomes challenging, so you'll want to be physically ready for this one before starting out. Legs will seldom get a rest, and many trees cross the trail, forcing you to climb over or crawl under them. The path is well marked near the bottom, but the blue blazes disappear as you go higher.

To reach the trailhead from Manchester, drive north on US 7. Take the first left onto Seminary Road. Follow it to the front of Burr and Burton Seminary. Continue on Seminary Road as it bears around to the left. Take the next right into the driveway that leads up behind the school into a large parking area.

Climb up to the athletic field above the parking area. Cross to the far side toward the left corner and watch for the well-beaten path. Unsigned but blue-blazed, the Burr and Burton Trail begins here.

The flat, needle-covered trail winds gradually upward beneath white pines. It joins an old road and continues straight. As the incline steepens, a yellow-blazed path exits left. The rutted road forks at .4 mile, and the trail goes left. Climbing the moderate slope, you switch back to the right and cross an intersecting road at .6 mile.

Thick stands of striped maple line the way. At the next fork (.7 mile), follow the trail left. Another path joins from the left rear before you bear right at the next fork.

You can now forget about watching for forks in the trail and turn your attention to the running ground pine along the path's edges. This creeping evergreen is actually a club moss. It is used for Christmas decorations and is commonly referred to as princess pine.

As the trail switches back to the left and loops widely right, its pitch increases. From here to the summit, you are in for a relentless uphill trek. Passing through many white birches, the path makes a long traverse up to the left. It narrows suddenly and squeezes past a glacial boulder at 1.3 miles. Quickly returning to its wider ways, it again climbs steadily.

Evergreens cloak the hillsides as the path begins a wide swing to the right. Footing becomes less sure as it narrows. The slope steepens even more. The sides of the trail rise as it turns right. This rock-filled shallow gully is a haven for lush greens. Mosses, lichens, and ferns fill the evergreen-shaded path.

After a series of short turns the trail makes a long, steep climb to the left. At 2.1 miles it ends the sharp uphill pitch and bends slowly right. It becomes surprisingly gradual before gaining elevation again.

Make your way up through body-brushing balsams past the "NO TRESPASSING" signs (these apply not to hikers but to hunters, trappers, and people carrying firearms). Just beyond, at 2.5 miles, several trails intersect. At the first fork bear left; at the second fork pass the red trail and follow the yellow trail. The next .2 mile to the summit passes through evergreens. You cross an old road at 2.6 miles and climb to the junction with the Lookout Rock Trail. Go left across the open ledge to the summit. Ahead is the Equinox Sky Line Inn.

By circling the inn you can see for miles in all directions. On the far horizon you can look into New York State, Massachusetts, and New Hampshire. On a clear day, Mont Royal in Montreal, Canada, is also said to be faintly visible.

Looking north and east you can see Dorset Peak, Killington Peak, Bromley Mountain, Magic Mountain, and Mount Ascutney. To the south, Stratton Mountain, Mount Snow, and Glastenbury Mountain are prominent. The Adiron-

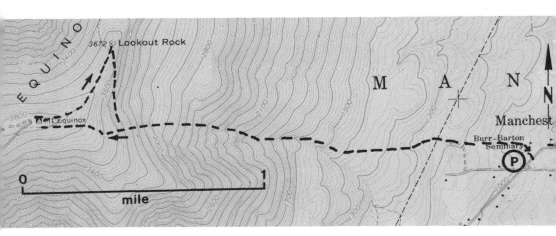

View from summit of Mount Equinox

dacks rise to the west.

Also located on the summit are Federal Aviation Agency peripheral communications stations. These radio towers enable planes to contact Boston's Logan Airport for landing instructions. An educational television station erected by the University of Vermont transmits near the Lookout Rock Trail.

When you are ready to descend, return to the Lookout Rock Trail and follow it .4 mile to Lookout Rock. This is a fairly easy walk over some rock and through evergreens. A small clearing along the way contains a memorial to Mr. Barbo, the dog of Dr. J.G. Davidson, former owner and developer of much land on Mount Equinox.

From Lookout Rock you gaze down into the Vermont Valley. Stratton Mountain looms to the right and Equinox Pond sits directly below you.

Leaving this vantage point, bear left onto the yellow trail and follow it .4 mile to the junction with the Burr and Burton Trail. Turn sharply left onto this unsigned trail and return via your original route to your car.

15

Bromley Mountain

Class: III
Distance (round trip): 4.6 miles
Hiking time: 2 1/2 hours
Vertical rise: 1,320 feet
USGS 15' Londonderry

This is a two-in-one hike. The greater part, two-thirds of the way up Bromley Mountain, is a gentle woodland walk. The last third is a steeper, slower climb. You can meander or stride for about 1.5 miles before settling into the more arduous, muscle-tugging final climb of .7 mile.

The trail to Bromley Mountain is maintained by the U.S. Forest Service, and begins at the Long Trail crossing of the Manchester-Peru Highway (VT 11). Drive east 5.9 miles from Manchester Center or west 4.4 miles from Peru. Turn north at the Green Mountain National Forest sign and park in the paved parking lot.

Walk approximately 150 yards down the road. At the sign for the Long Trail turn left into the woods. Follow the well-beaten path across the steel footbridge over Bromley Brook. The white-blazed trail leads very gradually upward. Cut logs carry you across a wet area as the ground flattens out. Step over the thin, weaving roots and small rocks that fill the path. Sounds of moving water can be heard to the left. As you continue, the rock-floored brook comes into view. Flashes of white water highlight its swirling, downward journey.

To the sides of the trail are the ever-present dead or dying trees that form an integral part of the forest's life cycle. They serve as hosts for various types of fungi—nonflowering plants that lack the chlorophyll necessary for photosynthesis and thus depend upon other organisms for food.

You can see examples of the rusty-hoof fome that attaches itself primarily to beech and birch trees. This three-to twelve-inch wide, cone-shaped fungus is a perennial that may grow for as long as thirty-five years. With each new year it adds a zone of tubes, called pore fungi, located on the plant's sheltered underside.

Walking gradually upward to the right, you reach another crossing of Bromley Brook at .6 mile. A raised, cross-logged footbridge provides rustic support here. Rising up from the brook, the trail becomes very flat as it winds through open woodlands. Occasional glacial boulders loom mutely among the trees, their great bulks harboring the many greens of ferns, mosses, and trees.

The way leads past a wide, gentle rock-free section of Bromley Brook on the right. A three-logged bridge carries you over a small streamlet on its way to the brook. As you pass through this area, you must step over several other trickles of water.

At 1.3 miles a small hump of ledge interrupts the flatness of the path. The bright whiteness of this quartz-filled rock contrasts sharply with the dull brown of the packed dirt path.

Watch for pleurotus mushrooms growing on living trees (they never grow on the ground). The oyster pleurotus grows in tight clusters and has three-to five-inch flared caps, one above the other. Gills form riblike undersides. This mushroom is usually white or grey when young and becomes yellowish with age. We do not recommend sampling any of the mushrooms described. Many edible and poisonous species look so much alike it is nearly impossible to tell them apart.

The trail approaches the brook again at 1.6 miles and then swings away to the left. Your first taste of the steep climb that will bring you to the top lies just ahead. After cresting a short ridge and temporarily leveling out, the path begins a serious ascent.

The way narrows as it begins the long climb. Thick birches, maples, and beeches staunchly guard the edges of the twisting trail. Huge boulders lean out from the hillside above as you climb diagonally to the right. Cresting the ridge, the path swings left across it and readies itself for the heights ahead. Rising steeply again, the trail passes through predominantly beech forests. It tops this ridge and flattens out once again.

The hairy woodpecker is common here. This black and white bird has a white breast and vertical stripes down its back. (The male displays a small red

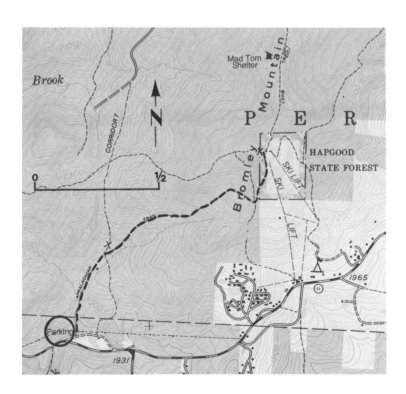

Bridge over Bromley Brook

patch on the back of his head.) Its barb-tipped tongue can be extended into holes to reach the larvae of boring beetles. Not to be confused with the smaller, but similarly marked downy woodpecker (six to seven inches long), the hairy woodpecker (eight to nine inches long), has a much longer, heavier bill, and it dwells primarily in forests.

Just before reaching a ski slope at 2.2 miles, the path crosses an unusual jumble of smooth-topped rocks. Look right (south) when you walk out onto the ski slope for a beautifully framed view of Stratton Mountain (elevation, 3,936 feet).

Turn left and follow the steep ski trail to the top of Bromley Mountain. A sturdy wooden observation tower offers fine views in all direction. Close to the north is Styles Peak. Looking east you see many low rolling hills, with no outstanding peaks. Stratton Mountain is prominent in the south, and the high peak in the distance to the southwest is Glastenbury Mountain. The Taconic Range looms impressively to the west. Hotel-topped Mount Equinox dominates the near west.

Your return will be by the same route.

16

Baker Peak and Griffith Lake

Class: III
Distance (round trip): 7.4 miles
Hiking time: 4 hours
Vertical rise: 2,130 feet
USGS 15' Wallingford

This hike takes you through an area that was quite exclusive in earlier times. Vermont's first millionaire, Silas Griffith, built a lake house retreat on the body of water that now bears his name. He made his fortune lumbering the forests around the nearby town of Danby, although the town itself did not take on an air of prosperity until quarrying and dairy farming became established in the 1800s.

Expansive views from the summit of Baker Peak and a peaceful visit to the wilderness shores of Griffith Lake highlight this outing. The mileage makes this trek a real leg-stretcher, but there are no sections of tedious climbing. Even the approach over open ledges to Baker Peak can be handled easily.

Drive 2 miles south from Danby on US 7. Turn east onto a paved road next to a small cemetery. Follow this road for .5 mile to the Green Mountain National Forest sign for the Lake Trail, on the left. There is ample parking in an open field beside the sign.

Your walk begins on the Lake Trail and then branches off onto the Baker Peak Trail. After leaving the summit of Baker Peak, you'll walk the Long Trail

south to Griffith Lake. The Lake Trail will return you to the parking area.

The blue-blazed Lake Trail leads right from the field where you parked and follows the old carriage road that leads from the valley to Griffith's lake retreat. Pine needles cloak the trail here as it leads gradually upward. You can hear the loud rushing of McGinn Brook below the hillside to the left. After the initial gradual incline the trail levels out, and at .2 mile it dips down to cross a fast-flowing brook, whose left bank it then parallels. Look for a piped spring on your left at .5 mile, after which the path makes a rounded switchback to the left (.6 mile). This is the start of a long upward traverse.

The hillsides rise high above and drop off steeply below. Smooth ledges form occasional walls above the trail. At 1.2 miles a bridge carries you across a gap beneath one of these steep stone faces. The supports of an old trestle can be seen imbedded in the rock below. Beyond the bridge the trail continues to traverse the slope. Steadily climbing, it narrows and passes along a hillside flooded with white birches.

The way swings right, still curling

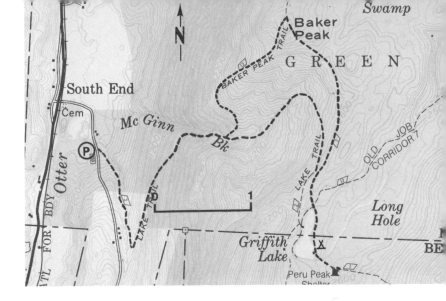

around the hillside's edge. McGinn Brook's gushing becomes audible far below, but its frothy white waters settle into quiet pools where the trail comes to meet the stream. You will soon find a spur trail on the right which leads 200 feet to a view overlooking Dorset Peak and the Route 7 valley. At 1.5 miles you reach Ben's Bathtub, one of the larger pools along the trail. This lovely spot invites you to refresh yourself before traveling on.

You reach a trail junction just after you cross McGinn Brook at 1.6 miles. The Lake Trail leads right and the Baker Peak Trail, left. Go left onto the blue-blazed Baker Peak Trail, which makes a long, moderate climb along the mountain's western slope. The narrow path passes between brilliant slopes of white birches and leads just below the ridge line. Then, swinging sharply right, it passes over rougher sections of loose rock and protruding roots. The trail becomes more gradual as it curves through thick stands of dwarfed birches.

At 2.4 miles you reach open ledge. Looking left you can see US 7 in the valley below. Dorset Peak, with its white quarries, rises commandingly beyond the highway. The quarries were first worked in the early 1800s. At that time the demand was for relatively small cut stones to be used for hearths, doorsteps, and tombstones. With the advent of better transportation and equipment, larger stones were quarried.

The Baker Peak and Long Trails join at 2.5 miles, and the final ascent is a steady climb over a wide, smooth spine of rippled ledge. To your left is a tantalizing preview of the wide western view you'll witness at the top.

Just beyond the summit, a sign marks Baker Peak's elevation at 2,850 feet. The view extends through 180 degrees of the compass. In clear weather, sharp-peaked Killington and the rounded cone of Pico can be seen to the north. The Adirondacks are partially visible to the northwest. Dorset Peak is directly across, with Woodlawn Mountain behind to the right. Emerald Lake sparkles to the south. Netop Mountain and Green Peak back it up, while Equinox Mountain raises its lofty head just beyond. In the valley, you see the town of Danby to the northwest. US 7 slices the valley floor in a north-south direction, and the looping bends to its east are Otter Creek.

Along the Lake Trail

Return to the junction of the Baker Peak and Long Trails. Go left onto the Long Trail South. This route is consistently easy going. Level stretches alternate with gradual dips and rises. At 3.3 miles you begin the first noticeable ascent as the path brushes by a large glacial boulder. At 3.6 miles you cross a damp, boggy area via the raised roots of nearby trees.

The Long Trail intersects with the Lake Trail at 4.3 miles and swings left. Follow It approximately 500 feet through evergreens and birches to the northern end of Griffith Lake. Sunlight dances on the water's surface as you approach. After passing the Old Job Trail on the left you reach the lake's shore. This quiet, primitive setting is an ideal spot to eat lunch and spend some time just lazing around.

Continuing on a series of board bridges, the Long Trail follows the eastern shore of Griffith Lake and in .2 mile passes several tent platforms. To protect this shoreline and preserve its natural beauty, all camping within 200 feet of Griffith Lake is restricted to these platforms, or to the Peru Peak Shelter .6 mile further south on the Long Trail. A GMC caretaker is in residence at the tenting area, and a small fee is charged for overnight use here and at the shelter.

When ready, retrace your steps on the Long Trail to its junction with the Lake Trail. Go straight on the blue-blazed Lake Trail. At 5.2 miles the trail bears left onto an old road, which it follows for approximately .5 mile down a long, gradual grade, crossing several tiny brooks in the process.

The road narrows to trail width as rushing brooks accompany it on both sides. They meet and swing left as the path crosses over them and shortly thereafter intersects the Baker Peak Trail. Go straight, across McGinn Brook, and follow your original route back to your car.

17

Mount Antone

Class: II
Distance (round trip): 4.6 miles
Hiking time: 2 1/2 hours
Vertical rise: 850 feet
USGS 7.5' Pawlet

Mount Antone lies within the boundaries of Merck Forest (see also Hike 2). This unique woodland and forest area contains twenty-six miles of hiking and cross-country ski trails for public use. Nine overnight shelters and many picnic sites are also scattered throughout the forest. There is no charge for visiting the forest, which is run by a private foundation, but contributions are appreciated. Any money received is applied to future recreational and educational goals. Visitors are requested to obey the forest's rules, however:

1. All visitors must register.
2. No motor vehicles are allowed beyond the parking area.
3. Camping is by permit only.
4. Fires are allowed only in designated areas.
5. All trash must be carried out.
6. Hunting and fishing are permitted, but kills must be reported.
7. Only snowshoers and cross-country skiers may use the forest in the winter.

The entrance to Merck Forest is located on VT 315 at the height-of-land between Rupert and East Rupert. Drive east 3.3 miles from the junction of VT

153 in Rupert, or west 2.6 miles from the junction of VT 30 and VT 315 in East Rupert. Turn south toward the brown and yellow ''Merck Forest Foundation, Inc.'' sign. When the entrance road forks, bear right and go .5 mile to the parking area, on the right.

Walk the short distance to the information board, and register. Maps of the forest are also available here. Now go through the log swing gate next to the information board and begin your hike down Old Town Road. White birches surround you as the road leads gradually upward. In about .2 mile you come to a junction—there's a large barn on the left. Bear right to stay on Old Town Road.

The trail dips between large patches of cleared land. Down to the right is Page Pond. You're likely to hear the quacking of wild ducks echoing from this tiny body of water. Just beyond the pond you can look up to the right and see the humped dome of Mount Antone. You head up a slight rise, where young trees begin to fill the hillside to the left. Open land to the right allows for an excellent view to the northwest.

Young forests cloak both sides of the trail as it continues to rise gradually and then flattens out. Continued easy walking brings you to a sweeping left turn at .8 mile. Follow the curve to the clearing, where several trails radiate outward. Before turning sharply right to follow the footpath leading to Mount Antone's summit, walk to the far edge of this cleared area. From here you can see Mount Equinox, with its summit hotel and transmitting towers.

Follow the grassy trail next to the Mount Antone Road sign. Look carefully; it's just off to the right when you reach the clearing. On the left you'll see a stand of red pines, with their characteristically uplifted branches. This northern tree has three-to eight-inch needles in clusters of two.

Gentle dips and rises make for easy walking as the trail passes through hardwood forests. Many thin, young hop hornbeams cover this area. At 1.1 miles you pass through Clark Clearing. Another clearing just beyond offers distant views west to the Adirondacks of New York State.

A quaint four-sided cabin comes into view on the right. Built of logs and set atop a stone foundation, it has tall, narrow windows fashioned by leaving out vertical logs in appropriate places. Stumps and flat stones make the inside comfortable, while a front overhang keeps rain from the open door.

In front of the cabin is a four-way trail junction. The Mount Antone Road leads upward. To the left is a ski-touring trail. The steeper part of the hike begins here. You cut up to the left across a slope and turn right. A series of turns brings you to the crest of the ridge. The trail remains smooth and easy to walk through here,

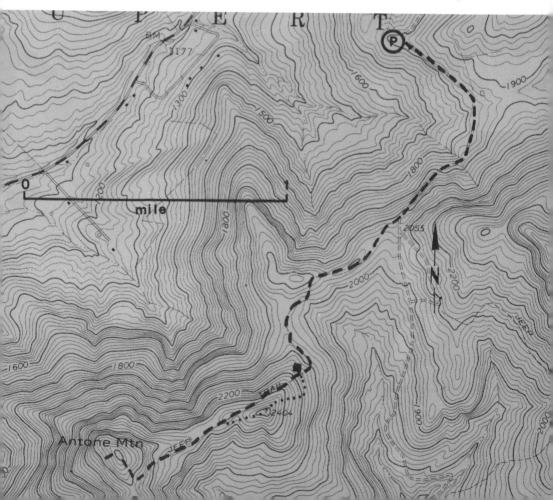

White birches

but the incline does offer some challenge.

The trail flattens out and crosses the ridge to the right. Just ahead, at 1.8 miles, the ski-touring trail rejoins from the right. Continue straight on the Mount Antone Road when the Wade Lot Road branches left. In another 500 feet you pass Lookout Road. The trail then bends around a small knoll on the right and begins a long, straight, gradual ascent.

At 2.1 miles you reach a sweeping switchback to the right. Leading left from the turn are the Beebe Pond Trail and Masters Mountain Road. The grade is now steeper as you climb to the summit.

You enter the small, flat area at the top of Mount Antone 2.3 miles from the information center. To the right (northeast) you overlook much of Merck Forest. The barn you passed earlier is visible in the large clearing straight ahead. The three towering summits beyond are (from right to left): Dorset Peak, Woodlawn Mountain, and Tinmouth Mountain.

A narrow path leads off the far side of the clearing. Follow this a short distance to another cleared overlook. From here you look down into the valley to the fields of scattered farms and out across low, rolling hills. On a clear day it is possible to see westward as far as the Adirondack peaks of Mount Marcy and Whiteface Mountain.

On the return trip, take the ski-touring trail, which branches off to the left after .5 mile. It descends moderately and straight along the side of the slope and will bring you back to the cabin. Remember to bear left here and then hike back to the information center by the route you came up. If you enjoyed this trek, why not plan to return to Merck Forest in winter for some excellent cross-country skiing?

18

Natural Bridge

Class: III
Distance (round trip): 3.2 miles
Hiking time: 1 3/4 hours
Vertical rise: 840 feet
USGS 7.5' Dorset

Imagine a deep gorge carved into solid rock by the relentless rushing of cascading water. Ragged edges show where rocks have broken away, and the sides of the crevice flare freely upward—with one exception. Somehow a slender span of rock has failed to crumble. It connects the sides of the gorge like a narrow catwalk. This is the natural bridge.

Don't be misled by the shortness of this hike. It is a rugged climb, which follows logging roads except for the last 100 yards, and is blazed with faded blue paint. The trail itself is easy to walk, but the steep incline keeps you leaning into the hill most of the way. Be ready for a good workout. However, the many breathers that your heart, lungs, and legs will insist upon, should provide excellent opportunities to observe the abundant plant and animal life of this area.

To reach the trailhead, turn west off US 7 in North Dorset onto the entrance road for Emerald Lake State Park. Drive into the park and leave your car in the parking area. You will be asked to pay a nominal fee. Walk back down the road .3 mile and turn left by the white and black state park sign to pick up the trail.

Please note: This trail is on private land, and the property owner has, so far, allowed the public to use it. This permission can be rescinded at any time, so hikers should help care for the path as they hike.

Climbing easily at first, the trail continues on an abandoned town road, passing two old dams in the brook to the left. At .3 mile, a blue-blazed old road forks to the left, and ascends through the state park to the old County Road. At this fork, keep right and ascend the steep logging road ahead.

Hemlocks arch their delicate branches along the path. These beautiful trees have more flexible twigs and branches than spruces or balsams, as well as tiny, perfectly formed cones. Their bark is rich in tannin; woodsmen and Indians made tea from the twigs and leaves. A barbed-wire fence parallels the path and seems to divide the forest. White birches abound to the right while evergreens occupy the left. The long, moderate uphill grade continues.

The logging road becomes steeper and the sides of the path rise higher; your steps become more laborious. Then you crest a long grade and swing sharply left. The grade lessens a bit as the trail makes a long, winding climb.

Looking left through the trees, you can see a ridge line towering high above across a deep valley. The mountains responsible for this high landmark are Dorset Hill, Netop Mountain, and Dorset Peak.

The trail swings sharply left as the hillside suddenly flattens out. The grade lessens. Your legs get a short reprieve.

Red squirrels may chatter at you throughout this area. These vivacious creatures have a very small home range—usually within a small group of trees. They live in hollow trees; or, if these are not available, they build outside nests of grass and fine twigs and line them with shredded bark. In addition to gathering nuts and cones for winter storage, they place mushrooms high on tree branches to dry in the sun before tucking them away.

You cross a dry brook bed at 1 mile. The trail cuts across the slope here and remains fairly flat. Deer tracks can be seen in the soft dirt. Whitetail deer most often leave separated, two-toed tracks, although sometimes they appear as single, heart-shaped prints. You may be fortunate enough to see one of these beautiful creatures or at least its raised white flag (tail) as it runs from you. A sharp snort or whistle will also signal the presence of deer. You will cross another brook at 1.1 mile.

Just before the trail begins to rise again, it passes by a jumble of large white limestone rocks. Ferns begin to appear along the sides of the trail. Two kinds grow abundantly here. The maidenhair fern with finely divided horseshoe-shaped leaves; and the Christmas fern, which is slender from base to tip with a scaly leafstalk, stiff leaves, and spiny leaflets.

You will reach a junction at 1.4 miles. Bear right, avoiding the blue-blazed road on your left, and the blue-blazed road straight ahead. After 100 yards, turn right at the fork. *Please note:* As of this writing, the blue blazes on the trail from this

point on have been painted over with black paint.

As you continue on this path, the presence of a stone wall on the right alerts you to the next turn. At the end of the wall, go steeply downhill to the right. The narrow path leads directly to the natural bridge. If you miss this trail turn-off, you will soon reach a brook crossing. Back-track 150 feet and look for the trail on your left at the end of the stone wall.

The two-foot-wide stone arch is starting to crumble, so do not try to walk out on it. It connects the rocky hillsides above the floor of the gorge. Water only flows here during the spring runoff.

Little Rock Pond and Green Mountain

Class: III
Distance (round trip): 5.6 miles
Hiking time: 4 1/2 hours
Vertical rise: 1,849 feet
USGS 15' Wallingford

Give yourself plenty of time to enjoy this wilderness pond and mountain. The area teems with wildlife, and you won't want to rush. A quiet wait can reward you with lots of animal sightings. And besides, it's nice to bask in the sun atop the ledges of Green Mountain.

If an overnight stay fits your plans, you can sleep at either the Lula Tye Shelter (located .2 mile from the southeast tip of Little Rock Pond), at Little Rock Pond Shelter (located .1 mile from the northern end of the pond), or at the designated tenting area on the pond's eastern shore. The heavy use this popular pond receives requires careful management to preserve its beauty and fragile shoreline environment. Camping within 200 feet of the pond's shoreline is restricted to designated sites on the east shore only. A GMC caretaker is in residence, and a small overnight fee is charged here and at the shelters.

You'll reach your destination via the Homer Stone Brook Trail. To get to it turn east off US 7 just south of the South Wallingford Union Congregational Church. Drive .2 mile across a bridge and around a right-hand curve to a red building on the left. This is the South Wallingford Youth Community Center.

Park beside it.

The Homer Stone Brook Trail begins behind the next house on the left. *Please note:* No parking is allowed near this house. Walk up the driveway and around to the right of the house.

The trail starts by following the old South Wallingford-Wallingford Pond Road. The way leads up a moderate grade, flanked by stone walls and open fields. Blue blazes and occasional arrows mark the route.

After .2 mile the road makes a wide swing to the right. Keep on this packed-dirt road and bypass the path leading left at the bend. Maintaining its gradual slope, the road leads up between borderling hemlocks. These evergreens dust the trail with their tiny needles and miniature cones.

Beyond the hemlocks, you pass through an open deciduous forest. A massive, gnarled maple guards the left side of the road as another trail leads left. Stay on the road. Walking is enjoyable up this gradual incline. You make a brief aromatic passage through a small area of hemlock and white pine.

After .6 mile you can hear the rushing waters of Homer Stone Brook below to the right. Follow the road as it bends right and passes by still another trail leading left.

Now the trail parallels the brook. Clear water pours through boulders trying to choke its flow. Rippled pools form among the rocks. Above to the left the hillside slopes steeply around eroded cliffs. Quaking and large-tooth aspen and beech cling tenaciously to the slope.

For a short stretch the brook drops down into a shallow ravine. You can hear it foaming and surging along below the road. Farther along, the road and brook parallel each other at the same level. A U.S. Forest Service sign points the way. At approximately 1.3 miles you cross the Homer Stone Brook, leaving the South Wallingford-Wallingford Pond Road. Rounded stones help you cross the flowing water.

Bear sharply right (avoiding the road on your left), after crossing the brook. Walk about 100 feet, turn sharply left,

and begin to climb up the gouged-out slope. Very quickly you top a small mound of earth while the trail joins with an old road. Turn left here. Mark this junction well so that you will not pass by it on the return trip.

The grassy road cuts upward and across the slope. Small rocks clutter the path and make progress slow at times. Homer Stone Brook again meets the trail near the top of this long incline. The trail crosses over the brook and reaches the junction with the Long Trail at 1.9 miles (Little Rock Pond Shelter is .1 mile north via the Long Trail). Go right and follow the white blazes toward Little Rock Pond. The blue-blazed Green Mountain Trail appears quickly on the right. Turn here and follow it over rough-hewn logs bridging the brook's northern outlet. Follow the blue blazes along the pond's western shore.

Little Rock Pond is a resting place for

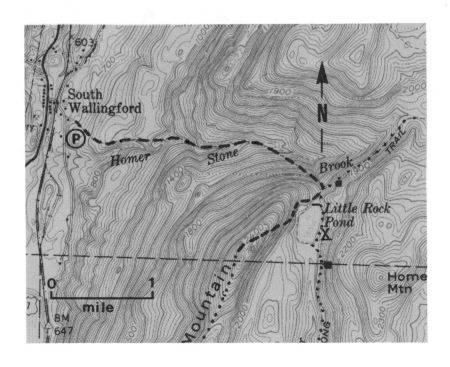

Mallards

mallards, Canada geese, and other waterfowl during their spring and fall migrations. Approach its shores with care and you may see one of these species before their wary senses make them fly off.

Mallards are bottom feeders. They submerge their upper bodies in shallow water in quest of plant growth. You will see them "tip up," with their tailends pointing skyward. Recognize the drake by his iridescent green head, white neck ring, white-edged blue wing patch, and curled tail feathers. The hen shares the blue wing patch but is dappled in shades of brown.

The large Canada goose has a black neck and a white mark running like a strap from ear to ear beneath its head. These birds feed on pond plants and on the grass or grain of open fields. In flight, they align themselves in various V formations. "Honking" usually signals the approach of their flying wedge long before you can see it.

The path gently dips and rises along the pond's western shore. Ahead you can see a small island. After you pass

the point of the pond's northern outlet, with the island still visible ahead of you, the blue-blazed trail to Green Mountain leads right, climbs a short steep slope, and passes the junction of the blue-blazed Little Rock Pond Loop Trail. You may choose to return to the Homer Stone Brook Trail by this route on your way back. This Loop Trail follows the pond shoreline .4 mile to the Long Trail at the southeast corner of Little Rock Pond. From here it is .4 mile via the Long Trail to the Homer Stone Brook Trail. Enroute you pass the designated tenting area and the caretaker's tent.

The ascent to Green Mountain is a circuitous, sometimes steep climb upwards. Multi-zoned polystictus (a fungus with a shape and coloration resembling turkey tails) flare from the surface of dead tree limbs at the sides of the trail. At 2.4 miles the trail passes the "Dragon's Back," a long rocky spine of ledge. The more adventurous hiker may follow the "spine," climbing over the continuing series of ledges, and rejoin the Green Mountain Trail at the ledge top. Here, there are intermittent views to the east from open ledged areas as the trail twists through thick, evergreen scrub growth.

At 2.8 miles the Green Mountain Trail bears sharply right. Continue straight ahead 300 feet to the summit, where you will look out onto Little Rock Pond, 700 feet directly below; the various peaks of the White Rocks National Recreation Area (east); and the Big Branch Wilderness Area (southeast).

Return by the same route to the Homer Stone Brook Trail (or take the alternate Little Rock Pond Loop Trail described above), and retrace your steps to your car.

White Rocks Cliff

Class: III
Distance (round trip): 3.2 miles
Hiking time: 2 hours
Vertical rise: 1,622 feet
USGS 15′ Wallingford

You are not at White Rocks Cliff when you reach the highest point of this hike. The spur trail to the cliff follows a rugged, .2-mile downhill route. Once there, you'll enjoy a vantage point with panoramic views to the north and west. There is also a near view of one of three distinct limestone rock slides below northwest face of White Rocks Mountain. About the turn of the century, water coursed down the mountain, causing one whole side to slide off.

Drive east on VT 140 from Wallingford. Bear right onto a side road after about 2 miles. Follow it 500 feet to the

sign for the "Green Mountain National Forest: White Rocks Picnic Area." Turn right here and proceed straight on this road for .4 mile to picnic area #52 and the parking lot at its end.

You want the blue-blazed Keewaydin Trail, which leads out of the parking lot's far end. This wide trail begins with a gentle walk between picnic tables and two small Forest Service structures. Off to the left you'll hear the sound of a rushing brook. *Please note:* A portion of the Keewaydin Trail may become part of the white-blazed Long Trail soon after this revision is printed. The route to White Rocks Cliff will remain the same, but may be blazed in white (not blue) until the White Rocks Cliff Trail is reached.

The trail swings right, up and away from the brook. White pine have shed their five-fingered needles across the path. After cresting a rise, you approach a stream and swing left before it.

Now you maintain a steady upward grade through white birch, largetooth aspen, oak, and maple. Below and to the left you can hear the brook again. Look small but very attractive cascade.

The trail swings right around a thick,

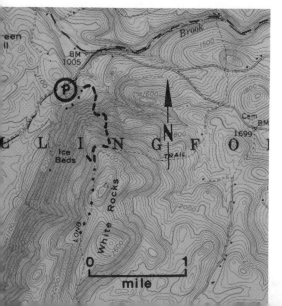

View of White Rocks Mountain and Cliffs

shadowy stand of spruce, balsam, and hemlock, and after briefly paralleling the ridge line to the left cuts up and across it. A short row of "bog logs" has been laid across a mucky section here.

Great glacial boulders loom in the open woods, and loose rocks fill the trail. Step slowly to avoid careless falls. The return to a packed-dirt trail makes the footing more certain. Your legs and feet appreciate this, as there are few other respites from the unvarying upward grade.

At 1.1 miles the Keewaydin Trail joins the Long Trail. Go right onto the Long Trail South. Frequent white blazes guide your way up and down the gentle dips and rises of the west side of a ridge. Stands of spruce and balsam seem to engulf you. Evergreen spills litter the path. You may want to pause along this sheltered trail to enjoy the surrounding quiet and isolation.

At 1.3 miles you reach a small clearing scattered with numerous broken rocks. The blue-blazed White Rocks Cliff Trail leads right. Make your way carefully over the loose rocks scattered down this steep, rugged descent.

The trail changes to packed dirt and continues its steep drop through conifers whose needles color the slope brown. Twisting and turning through large boulders and ledge, the path makes a final descent to the cliff.

Here there are two flat overlooks: one to the north and one to the west. The town of Wallingford is most prominent to the right. Tinmouth Mountain rises straight ahead in the first ridge line. The second, higher ridge line is that of the Adirondacks of New York State.

Directly below you is one of the great white limestone spills. This type of rock is still processed in a nearby plant. It is used as a base for toothpaste and as an ingredient in lead-base paint.

After returning to the parking area via the same route, you may want to explore the White Rock Trail. This blue-blazed path leads southwest from the other end of the parking lot to an outcropping of ledge below White Rocks Cliff. From this vantage point you can see the cliff and all three white rivers of rock that cascaded down the mountainside. The round-trip walk on this .5-mile-long switchbacking trail takes ½ hour.

21

Mount Ascutney

Class: III
Distance (round trip) 6.4 miles
Hiking time: 3 hours
Vertical rise: 2,400 feet
USGS 15' Claremont, NH–VT

Mount Ascutney has long been a focus of activity. During the French and Indian Wars bounties up to £100 were paid by both the English colonies and the French for enemy scalps. Colonial scalping parties frequented the area around Mount Ascutney and used to climb to its summit to watch for smoke from Indian campfires.

In 1825 the people of Windsor opened the first trail up the mountain—making Ascutney the first American mountain to have an established hiking trail. Later trails and shelters provided sufficient inspiration for James P. Taylor to found the Green Mountain Club and to initiate the blazing of the 262-mile Long Trail. The Long Trail prompted others to create the 2,000-mile Appalachian Trail, which stretches from Maine to Georgia.

Today, Ascutney boasts a 4-mile-long road to the summit (it is said to be one of New England's most scenic highways) and many ski trails. Small-plane and glider pilots use its distinctive shape as a convenient landmark.

To reach the Brownsville Trail, maintained by the Ascutney Trails Association, drive 5.2 miles west on VT 44 from its junction with US 5 in Windsor. You will spot a sign marking the start of the trail

just opposite a brick farmhouse on the right. White blazes mark the trail as it follows a long, flat, path past a sheep pasture which is surrounded by a high-intensity electric fence. The trail passes over private land here, and the owner requests that all dogs be kept on a leash.

Entering the woods the trail suddenly narrows and slithers through thick stands of hemlock. The branches overlap above, forming a natural tunnel. You follow a moderate grade up the mountainside, to a short, very steep section just before the trail joins the Norcross Quarry road. It rises gradually over packed dirt and loose stones. Then the hillsides become very steep to both left and right.

Slabbing the mountain, you cross a jumble of rocks flowing down over the trail like a stone waterfall, and continue upward through more hemlock. The incline lessens here but the footing is less certain as the path becomes filled with loose stones. Water trickles over the section of ledge to your left, all year long, forming a giant sheet of ice during the winter months. During the spring runoff it becomes a gorgeous waterfall.

Farther along (1.1 miles) you will recognize Norcross Quarry by the masses of large rock along the trailsides. Climb the pile to the right for a view of valleys, rolling ridges, and distant peaks. The long, thick wooden remains of a derrick and rusted steel cables evoke the past.

The Norcross Quarry was the most extensive of the four quarries on Mount Ascutney. It produced the sixteen polished columns for the Columbia University Library and the thirty-four large columns for Canada's Bank of Montreal. During its several years of operation, however, it did not produce stone completely free of trace iron. Thus, the stone did not weather well, and the quarry's backers went bankrupt.

The trail continues beneath overhanging ledge. It winds steeply upward between more hunks of ledge and turns sharply left and then right. It becomes steeper as thick stands of evergreens gather along the edges.

Soon, a short blue-blazed spur trail leads onto Quarry Top Lookout, a flat ledged area above Norcross Quarry. From here you have a wide view to the north. Return to the main trail. Climbing steadily through the woods, the trail nears a ski trail at 1.6 miles. Here the trail swings sharply to the left and climbs a series of diagonal traverses up the slope to Knee Lookout (2 miles), with a view to the east. Continue to twist and turn another .3 mile up the mountain until you reach a flat grassy area. This is North Peak: elevation 2,660 feet.

Just beyond this peak you have occasional views to the west through dead trees. Particularly prominent to the northwest are the pointed peak of Killington and the cone of Pico.

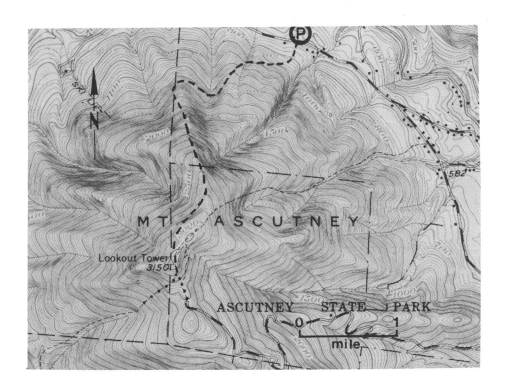

View to Mount Ascutney across the Windsor-Cornish bridge

Trees shorten as you climb steadily upward toward Mount Ascutney's 3,150-foot summit. At 2.9 miles you reach the junction of the Windsor Trail. Keep right.

The Stone Hut remains occupy the clearing 500 feet further on. You can still see the large slabs of granite used to construct the former shelter. Built in 1858 by volunteers, it was destroyed by vandals, rebuilt in the early 1900s, but later destroyed again—primarily by college students, who carved their initials in the metal roof with pistol bullets.

Leading to the right from this clearing is Brownsville Rock. From here you have a long view to the west and north. Open farmlands sectioned off by trees rise to mountain bases. Mount Mansfield and Camel's Hump are visible far to the north, while the Coolidge Range shows up clearly almost straight ahead. A bit south is Shrewsbury Peak. Salt Ash and Okemo mountains are the closer peaks to the left.

Return to the clearing and go right .2 mile to the summit. A lookout tower and accompanying horde of antennae greet you as you crest the last ledge area. Climb the tower for a fine 360-degree view of the surrounding countryside. Return to your car following the same route.

22

Quechee Gorge

Class: II
Distance (round trip): 1.5 miles
Hiking time: 1 hour
Vertical rise: 125 feet
USGS 7.5' Quechee

Quechee Gorge, Vermont's "Little Grand Canyon," was carved by the waters of the Ottauquechee River. In the middle 1800s the gorge and a nearby area with a steep grade impeded construction of the Woodstock Railroad, planned to link White River Junction and Rutland. Finally, in 1875, twenty-eight years after the Woodstock Railroad was originally chartered, ways were found to overcome these two natural barriers: passengers were enlisted to help push the train cars up the incline, and the gorge was spanned by a 282-foot trestle, crossing 165 feet above the river.

For years the Woodstock Railroad trestle was the highest railroad bridge in New England. Now recycled, it is used as the US 4 highway bridge, crossing the gorge 6 miles east of Woodstock and 5 miles west of White River Junction. The view from the highway bridge can be easily reached by car, but it will be far more rewarding after a walk along the Quechee Gorge Trail.

On US 4, .3 mile east of the gorge, you will see the sign for the Quechee State Park entrance. Turn into the entrance on the south side of the road and proceed along the dirt road for .2 mile.

Park your car at the small area on the right near a big shed which is filled with firewood. The Quechee Gorge Trail begins directly behind the woodshed. Blue blazes mark the way. (Please note that here, as at most Vermont state parks, all dogs must be kept on a leash.)

A delicious pine odor engulfs you momentarily as you approach the trail but disappears quickly as the pines are replaced by hemlocks. Tiny cones and red-brown needles blanket the flat meandering woodland trail.

At approximately .2 mile the trail veers sharply to the right and descends a steep grade through stands of white birch and hemlock. You will drop into a gully (.3 mile) where a side trail comes in on your right. Continue straight on the path.

Soon you cross over a brook with a split log bridge. After climbing out of the gully, the trail drops and again crosses the brook, using a larger log bridge. Notice the large dead trees on your left. These trees were killed when a family of beavers built a dam in the brook several years ago and flooded the area. The water's whispery gurgle interrupts the quiet of the glen. Roots traversing the trail form natural steps down to the water. Beyond the stream the path rises steeply once again, bearing sharply to the right at the top of the grade.

Soon the trail joins an old narrow grassy road and makes a ninety-degree turn to the left. After only a few steps, you can hear the din of the Ottau-quechee coursing through the gorge. Walk several hundred yards and you will reach a T junction in the trail. The gorge is straight ahead, and a chain link fence parallels the chasm for safety. Turn right here, and head up the wide road back towards US 4. Soon you will see the blue trail marker leading sharply into the woods on the right. This will be your return route. Continue straight on the road .2 mile, however, for a look at the gorge from the top. You pass under the bridge and almost immediately climb at a

reverse forty-five-degree angle (right) up to US 4.

Peering into the gorge on the north side can give you a dizzy feeling. Hemlock, pine, and maple grip the sides of this jagged slashway and funnel your gaze downward. The Ottauquechee River courses lavalike along the bottom of this deep cleft. Stretches of fast water scratch the dark surface with white.

Cross the bridge to the other side. The gorge appears much straighter and narrower here. The river moves faster and has molded deep impressions into the rocks.

Retrace your steps on US 4, around the gift shop, and back down under the bridge. Watch for the blue marker on your left.

The return trail eases back into the deeper woods and meanders parallel to

and below US 4. The quiet softness of the forest is shattered intermittently by the droning of automobiles.

You pass over a small stream with assistance from fallen logs and continue up a short steep hill which levels off in a grove of white pine. After a short dip, the trail bears left, and climbs a hill. Here, a trail comes in on your right. Continue straight ahead and begin a steep ascent through a hillside of dense hemlock.

The trail becomes quite steep as it climbs up to the circular park road at campsite #15. Go left and wind around the road. You will see rest rooms on your left, and your car is directly across the field. You may now either continue a short distance along the road or take the little path straight across the open field to your car.

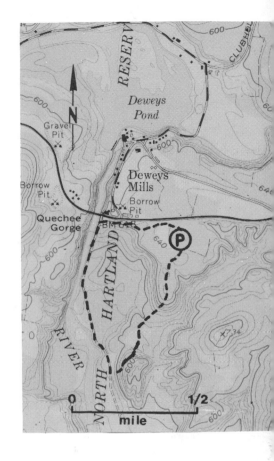

Mount Tom

Class: II
Distance (round trip): 2.4 miles
Hiking time: 1 1/2 hours
Vertical rise: 640 feet
USGS 7.5' Woodstock North

Traditionally, when the citizenry of Woodstock become concerned about some aspect of their town, action is sure to follow. Concern that the town's natural setting might be lost through development has led to the creation of three public parks inside the town's limits. Two of these, Billings Park on Mount Tom on the north side of town, and Mount Peg, just south of the village, are on tracts that were donated outright to the town. The Woodstock Park Commission is responsible for overseeing these two properties. The third, Faulkner Park, also on the north side of town and adjacent to Billings, is open to the public, but is owned and managed by the trustees of the Faulkner estate.

This loop hike from the village to the two peaks of Mount Tom uses the trail system of Billings Park, with the exception of one small segment of the Faulkner Trail, which a spur links with one of the Billings Park trails. Billings Park was given to the town in 1953 in the memory of Mary M. Billings French by her children. It has been left in its natural state except for the areas immediately next to the trails and a small plot around a Girl Scout cabin. The 155-acre tract extends from River Street,

on the north side of the Ottauquechee River, up the rugged, rocky south slope of Mount Tom, and north across the summit area. There are some magnificent views from the two peaks.

To reach the start of this hike from the village green in the center of Woodstock on US 4, walk or drive through the Union Street covered bridge and turn right onto River Street. The trail begins just past the River Street cemetery, on the left a short distance from the bridge.

The trail starts as a gently sloping, winding bridle path. Within .3 mile you come to the Girl Scout cabin on your left. Just beyond it, the trail to the summit of Mount Tom angles sharply to the left (sign to "North Peak Trail").

You will not have been long on this trail when you reach the first of two Link Trails to the Faulkner Trail. Bear right at this junction (sign here is to "Precipice Trail") and continue to the next, which is .2 mile from the cabin. The uppermost route on your left here is the Link Trail that you will use on your return.

Again bearing right (and following another "Precipice Trail" sign), you climb across the slope of Mount Tom. Just beyond a sharp switchback (where an

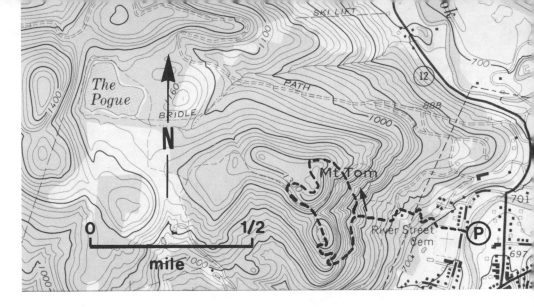

unblazed trail comes in from the right), you meet the North Peak Trail, which angles off to the right. There is a sign to "North Peak" and a somewhat faded curved yellow arrow painted on a rock in the trail.

You have now traveled .6 mile from River Street. The rocky bluff of Mount Tom stretches upward directly before you.

Bear right onto the North Peak Trail, which is about .5 mile long. (For a shorter walk, proceed straight ahead on the Precipice Trail to the South Peak, and then follow the return directions in the last paragraph.) The way leads at first steeply and then more gradually up the shoulder of Mount Tom. After a sharp turn to the left, the North Peak Trail joins the Back Loop Trail, which comes in from the right, and continues to the summit itself. The North Peak of Mount Tom is 1,320 feet above sea level and roughly 640 feet higher than the village. There are views from here south and west.

Just beyond the summit, the trail forks. Take the left fork, and follow this trail to an old carriage road leading to Mount Tom's South Peak.

Bear left and follow the old road .3 mile as it dips down and then up to the South Peak. Although this peak is the lower of the two (1,240 feet), the views are more impressive. Below, the Ottauquechee River winds through the village of Woodstock and the green fields of farms to the east.

Your route from here back into the valley is by way of the Faulkner Trail — look for the sign to "Mountain Avenue." Well defined, it cuts steeply down the face of Mount Tom for less than .1 mile before taking a zigzagging course that lessens the gradient considerably. In .4 mile you will reach the upper Link Trail on your left. Take it unless you wish to continue on down the Faulkner Trail to Mountain Avenue. After following the upper Link Trail for nearly .2 mile, a connector trail leading to the lower Link Trail goes off to the right. Keep left here, and after about 150 feet you will come to the trail to the Girl Scout cabin. Turn right and retrace your steps to your car. (If you have taken the Faulkner Trail all the way down, turn left on Mountain Avenue, which leads directly to the covered bridge.)

24

Amity Pond Natural Area

Class II
Distance (round-trip): 2.6 miles
Hiking time: 1 3/4 hours
Vertical rise: 660 feet
USGS 7.5' Woodstock North

In 1969 Elizabeth and Richard Brett deeded this land to the state of Vermont to be used for hiking, snowshoeing, cross-country skiing, and horseback riding. No motor vehicles are allowed here. Even radios are prohibited. The Amity Pond Natural Area is a place to refresh your senses and spirit.

Fires are permitted only at the shelters. Hikers are asked to remain on the trails to avoid any possible damage to the area. Picking or cutting flowers, plants, or trees is also not allowed.

From Woodstock drive north on VT 12 for 1.2 miles. As the road forks, bear right toward South Pomfret. Stay on this road for 2 miles to another fork at the South Pomfret Post Office. Go right toward Pomfret. Drive for 4.7 miles and then go left onto a paved road at the sign for I-89 just after the sharp bend to the right. After .3 mile turn left at another fork onto a dirt road. Drive 2.2 miles and look for the entrance to the Amity Pond Natural Area.

The absence of large signs is in keeping with the area's philosophy. Watch carefully for the blue and orange diamond-shaped trail markers and a small yellow poster on a tree on the left side of the road. There is limited park-

ing across the road from the entrance. The trail begins in an open area planted with red pine. A short spur leads immediately left to the rustic Amity Pond Shelter, where trail maps are available. The shelter faces a temporary pond, part of a water conservation experiment.

Return to the main trail and follow its wide, flat, grassy path. The blue and orange diamonds guide you along. You soon enter a rolling hilltop meadow punctuated by clumps of small trees and juniper. The meadow offers excellent views from the height-of-land. You can look to the south from here and see the saddle-backed hump of Mount Ascutney. The view to the west takes in the high, pointed top of Killington and the cone-shaped summit of Pico. To the right is tiny Amity Pond itself, hidden among recent growth of trees and shrubs.

An interesting tale describes how the pond got its name. Two girls who attended the East Barnard school together became chums and promised each other "friendship forever." When one married a man from the town of Pomfret and the other wed a man from Barnard, it was difficult for them to get together. So, by mail, they arranged to share a basket lunch on specified days at the grassy hill beside this tiny pond, which thus became known as Amity Pond.

The footpath winds gently down through the meadow. A hundred yards or so from the height-of-land leave the path and bear west through berry patches to the far right of the field. You will soon pick up a faint trail and see an opening in the woods. Passing between sections of an old stone wall, the trail enters the hardwood forest. Wide, flat and easy to walk, the trail bends to the right and meanders gradually down through the woods. After .6 mile you enter a small meadow where a spur leads left to the Sugar Arch Shelter.

Now grassy, the way passes beneath power lines and continues steadily downward. Thick stands of hemlock and occasional pines and spruces line the trail and a small brook parallels it to the left.

Just short of the 1-mile mark you step out into a huge open field. To the right are a church and cemetery; to the left, a farm house. Make your way across the open area to the road straight ahead.

Turn left onto the road and walk past a second farmhouse on the left. Just beyond, you cross the cement-sided road bridge over Broad Brook. Approximately 60 feet beyond the bridge the trail leads left off the road. It drops down through shrubbery to a trail sign and the brook.

Be alert for animal signs along the water and in damp areas ahead. A rac-

Amity Pond

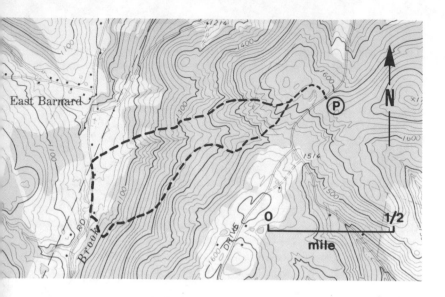

coon's imprint is particularly distinctive. Its front and hind feet have a pad with five slender toes. The tracks are usually paired with the left hind foot placed beside the right fore foot.

Rock hop across Broad Brook and continue up into the woods (ignore the short spur to the left just after the brook). Evergreens canopy the trail as the orange and blue markers lead you beside the brook for a short distance. Swing left and climb the moderate grade beside a barbed-wire fence. After a series of upward twists and turns, the path crosses a small stream via slim, cut logs.

After 2 miles a trail joins from the left. Continue straight here. A stone wall parallels the route as you climb steadily upward. The path flattens out and

passes beneath power lines. It then drops down a moderate grade to the bottom of a narrow gully and crosses over a trickling brook at 2.2 miles.

Beyond the brook you ascend a steep incline to the right. Near the top of this open-wooded slope you enter a small, round clearing. The trail swings sharply left and climbs to the top of a hill lined by a sparkling stand of white birches.

Cresting this rise, you step out into the southwestern corner of the meadow where Amity Pond is located. Follow the orange and blue markers up through the meadow to the height-of-land, rejoining the trail you were on before beginning the downhill leg of the loop. From here, retrace your steps back to your car.

25

Slack Hill

Class: II
Distance (round trip): 3.1 miles
Hiking time: 1 3/4 hours
Vertical rise: 542 feet
USGS 7.5' Plymouth

The leisurely woods walk to Slack Hill's summit takes you through the 3,400-acre Bradley Hill area of the rambling Calvin Coolidge State Forest, which covers 12,000 acres and is divided into several separate parcels. Whether you're camping at the park or are here for the hike only, you'll enjoy the wide trails, gradual slopes, and open wooded area. Allow plenty of time for an unhurried, relaxing, and beautiful walk.

From Bridgewater Corners drive south 4.2 miles on VT 100A to the entrance of the Calvin Coolidge State Forest. (Plymouth, the tiny community where Calvin Coolidge was born, is 2 miles further south. The Coolidge Homestead is open to the public.)

Follow the long, winding road from the park entrance to the Contact Station (admission and information booth). Pay the 75¢ per-person charge for day use of the facilities and park in the area to the right. If you are taking dogs along for the walk, remember to bring their leashes, as Vermont State parks do not allow dogs to run loose.

The blue-blazed trail begins behind and to the right of the booth. A longer trail (see map) begins back nearer the entrance of the park. However, it is used primarily as a pulp road—timber is harvested to insure proper management of trees and other vegetation—and does not have the scenic appeal of the foot-path.

Your route is divided into three separate sections. The gradual climb around Slack Hill is 1.3 miles long. A descent of .9 mile brings you to the parking lot at the picnic area. Another downhill walk of just under 1 mile along the road connecting the picnic area with the Contact Station will return you to your car.

The wide packed-dirt trail leads gradually upward through thin young trees. Occasional clumps of fern and slender striped maple provide the only major ground cover between the tree trunks. After topping the incline, the path levels and begins a series of short dips and rises. The trail becomes so wide open that it is possible to wander off the path. Keep an eye on the frequent blue blazes.

After .5 mile an arrow points to the right for a short trail back to the Contact Station and woodshed. Follow the blue blazes sharply left here. This area supports a wide variety of animal life. You might be lucky enough to see any of the following: chipmunks, red squirrels, partridge, woodcock, deer, or rabbits. Songbirds also flourish, particularly the inquisitive chickadee. To attract the black-capped chickadees try kissing the back of your hand or whistling chick-a-dee-dee-dee.

The trail begins to slab gradually across the hillside. It continues to pass through typical hardwood forests, which have only a scattering of the elms that were once prominent in them. The American elm seeds are eaten by grouse, squirrels, and opossum. Deer and cottontail rabbits browse the twigs. Unfortunately, this familiar tree is rapidly succumbing to Dutch elm disease.

After passing between thick stands of white birch, the path drops through a wide open area and joins a spur trail from the left. A sign here points left to Blueberry Lean-to. Swing sharply right.

Unusual clumps of maidenhair fern appear to the right of the trail. The finely divided leaves are four to sixteen inches wide and shaped like horseshoes. Individual leaves look like feathers in an Indian headdress as they waver in the slightest breeze.

Along the trail

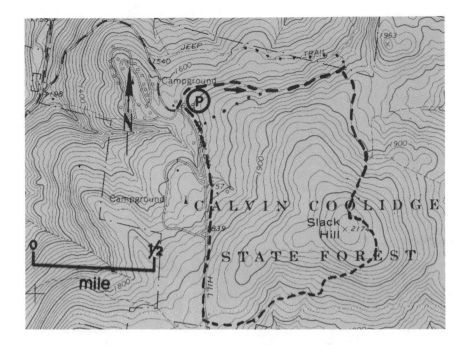

The trail winds across the hillside and at the 1-mile point steps over an old stone wall. It becomes narrower and climbs toward the summit. Thick stands of red spruce and carpets of wavy broom moss flank the path.

The ground levels as you come to the summit. A brown sign marks the spot. There are no views from here but you enjoy a peaceful relaxed feeling as you meander through evergreens.

Follow the blue blazes past the elevation sign and descend gradually .9 mile to the picnic area. Single logs imbedded diagonally in the dirt occasionally cross the trail. This is a system of erosion prevention that directs rain and snow runoff to the sides of the trail and keeps the flat path in fine condition.

Nearing the picnic area the trail switches back to the right. It winds between a thick area of white birches and red spruces. Glimpses of parked autos through towering white pines signal the end of the woodland trail. When you reach the paved park road, go right and follow it .9 mile to your car.

Shrewsbury Peak

Class: II
Distance (round trip): 3.6 miles
Hiking time: 2 1/2 hours
Vertical rise: 1,757 feet
USGS 7.5' Killington Peak

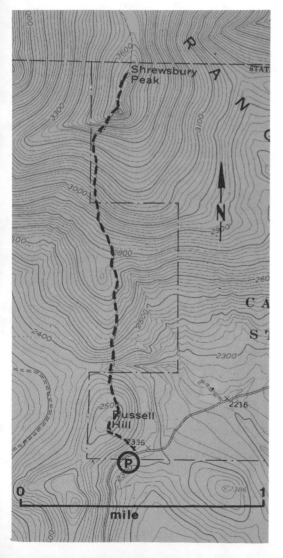

You leave the clutches of civilization before beginning this hike. No horns or screeching tires pierce the quiet as you start the roller-coaster-like climb to Shrewsbury Peak. With each step the quiet of the forest grows deeper. Evergreen tunnels diminish thoughts of the world you left behind. Silent mountains await your company at the summit.

Take VT 100 from either West Bridgewater or Plymouth Union to the dirt road leading west, .2 mile south of the tip of Woodward Reservoir. This road can be recognized by its exceptionally wide entrance beside the brown post and wire guard rails of VT 100. Follow it 3.3 miles to the short dirt road that leads to the former Northam Picnic Area. (Just before reaching this turn there will be a narrow dirt road on the right. Go past it and take the next right.) Park in the area in front of the shelter. The blue-blazed Shrewsbury Peak Trail is maintained by the Farm and Wilderness Foundation Camps and begins behind and to the left of the shelter.

You'll notice unusual trees beside the trail with dense conical shapes reaching almost to the ground. Scalelike leaves one-eighth of an inch long or less hug the twigs and branchlets of the flattened sprays. The bark is very fibrous, with many cross ridges. This tree—the northern white cedar—is a stranger to most of the hiking trails in this book. The northern white cedar grows in limestone soils and swamps, where it provides a favorite winter yarding food for deer. Moose, snowshoe hares, and cottontail rabbits also eat the twigs and foliage. Songbirds and red squirrels devour the seeds.

The trail swings around an old well. This water is not safe to drink. A sign here indicates you are 1.8 miles from Shrewsbury Peak.

Follow the moderate slope upward to the left. At .2 mile you reach a log lean-to with a bunk area tucked up under its short front overhang. A stone fireplace highlights this cozy, primitive dwelling. There is also an outhouse.

The path continues gradually to the top of Russell Hill, elevation 2,540 feet. It levels out and then descends a gentle slope past moss-covered glacial boulders.

At .4 mile you look down into a ravine and then begin the steep descent to its bottom. Once there, the only way is up as you follow the blue blazes over the boulder-strewn hillside. After cresting the ravine slope the trail becomes more gradual. It leads over, around, and between a long series of rocks and boulders. Many are covered with wavy brown moss.

The path crosses an old grassed-in road. It makes a short climb and then levels out for a short distance through beech trees and more boulders. After winding steadily but moderately upward, the path flattens out once again. For a surprisingly long way, it meanders over rock-and-root-free ground. Then, a long sloping upward climb reminds you that you are still heading for Shrewsbury Peak. Yellow birches appear to the left. Less striking than their white cousins, these trees have a creamy yellow or silver grey bark that peels in thin curls. Broken twigs give off a wintergreen odor.

You cross a dry brook bed at 1.3 miles (it will have water after a heavy rain). Here, the trail bears right and begins a steeper climb.

Thick, low balsams and red spruces begin to line the trail amid towering white birches. The balsam has long, flat, bright-green needles with two parallel silver stripes underneath. The red spruce has shorter needles that spiral closely around hairy twigs.

At approximately 1.4 miles you begin to see red blazes on some trees along the trail. These denote the boundaries of the Calvin Coolidge State Forest, through which this part of the Shrewsbury Trail now travels. The double blue blazes on occasional trees indicate a sharp turn.

The path now becomes more cluttered with roots and rocks. It twists and turns through evergreen fragrance and becoming steeper, begins its final ascent to the summit.

Thick evergreens brush your body as you climb up over larger rocks and moss-covered ledge. Winding up through a long evergreen tunnel, you pass two overlooks on the right with views to the south.

The 3,720-foot summit is a small, ledged clearing with a wide view to the south and east. Blue arrows on the rock point in two directions. (The trail can be followed for another 2 miles to a junction with the Long Trail.)

Looking straight ahead (southeast) from the ledge you see the two-pronged summit of Mount Ascutney beyond the second ridge. New Hampshire mountains form the horizon. Just left (east) of Mount Ascutney is Mount Kearsarge, elevation 2,937 feet. Far to the right of Ascutney (south-southeast) is Monadnock Mountain, elevation 3,165 feet. Swinging in a chain to the south are closer Vermont mountains. Smith Peak and Ingalls Hill lead up to dual-peaked Burnt Mountain. Beyond are Bear and Salt Ash mountains. This splendid panorama is a marvelous backdrop to a picnic lunch.

Your return trip follows the same route back to your car.

Snow-dusted route to Shrewsbury Peak

27

Killington Peak

Class: III
Distance (round trip): 6.8 miles
Hiking time: 4 1/4 hours
Vertical rise: 2,531 feet
USGS 7.5' Killington Peak, USGS 7.5' Rutland

At 4,241 feet, Killington is the second highest mountain in Vermont (only Mount Mansfield rises higher), and it is certainly one of the most popular. It's a four-season peak, with teeming ski slopes in winter and lots of good hiking the rest of the year. And (weather permitting) the views are magnificent.

There are several ways to reach the top. For those who desire comfort, the gondola and main chairlift reach to within a short walk of the summit. But if you're more athletically inclined, the Bucklin Trail offers a nice combination of flat walking on old logging roads and steeper, more strenuous climbing over rocks. The 6.8-mile round trip is long enough for a challenge, yet short enough to allow plenty of time atop the mountain.

The trail, maintained by the Killington Section of the GMC, begins at Brewers Corners on the Wheelerville Road. After you pass through Mendon on US 4 going east, take the first right (beyond a cement road bridge) onto the green-signed Wheelerville Road. Follow it exactly 4 miles to a sharp bend to the right. This is Brewers Corners. The trail begins on the left just before the bend. The blue blazes

and sign are just in off the road. Following an old logging road, you pass beneath towering pines, balsams, and spruces. The roar of water can be heard to the left as you leave the conifers and enter the hardwood forest.

Shortly you come to Brewers Brook. Cross it via the heavy wooden bridge that lists sharply to the right. The road begins a very gradual climb but continues to be easy to walk. The woods thin out as the hillsides slope upward above you to the right.

At .8 mile the road stops where two branches of the brook meet. Cross to the middle grassy area and then follow the brook up to the left. Step carefully along this very rocky section. About .2 mile farther along, the path meets slow-flowing water and crosses over it. Blue blazes mark the way to the continuation of the logging road on the other side.

Now on the north side of the brook, you quickly cross one of its small tributaries. The grade begins to increase slightly as goldenrod closes in from the sides. At approximately 1.7 miles, red markers cross the trail and stretch into the woods on both sides. These are the boundary markers for the Calvin

Coolidge State Forest. Just beyond, the trail forks and the blue blazes lead you to the right.

The pleasantly flat logging road now gives way to moderate slopes strewn with loose rocks. The trail narrows and winds upward through thin trees. Occasional openings to the left enable you to see towering companion peaks.

Winding upward to the right, the path becomes much greener along the edges. Hay-scented ferns swarm over the ground. Broom moss, wood sorrel, and shining club moss cluster around the bases of trees.

At approximately 2.3 miles, the trail crosses an old grassed-in logging road and continues upward through white birches which are quickly replaced by evergreens. The path flattens out a bit before swinging upward again to the right through thick stands of conifers. Note that you have just left the north side of the ridge and are now climbing straight up the slope in a southerly direction.

Red osier dogwood brushes against your legs and fills a large clearing to the left. This shrub is common throughout northern New England. Its branches spread loosely along the ground and rise no higher than six feet at the tips. The leaves are prominently veined, nearly smooth underneath, and pale. It bears dark red branches in winter and small white flowers in flat-topped clusters in June.

At 3.2 miles you reach an intersection and go left toward (clearly visible) Cooper Lodge. The trail winds sharply right just before the lodge and joins the Long Trail South for approximately 100 feet as far as a clearing. The Long Trail bears right here, and you continue straight ahead up the .2-mile spur to Killington Peak.

Rocks and small boulders fill the blue-blazed trail as it veers right at a fork. A tumble of rocks and ledge makes the climbing more difficult. Hands become as useful as feet here. Passing upward through scrub growth, you reach the open-ledged summit.

The mountaintop is surprisingly, and

View of Killington's summit, with Pico Peak beyond

disappointingly, civilized. A lookout tower and radio installation greet you first. On a short spur trail to the east is the Killington Gondola Terminal and Restaurant.

(In 1763, Rev. Sam Peters, a Connecticut clergyman, rode through central Vermont on a preaching and baptizing mission. He claimed to have christened the state "Verd-Mont," from the summit of Killington.)

From various points you can see to the distant horizons in all directions.

Pico Peak rises to the immediate north. Green Mountain peaks are visible north to Mount Mansfield and south to Glastenbury Mountain. The city of Rutland nestles in a long valley to the west, and beyond are the Taconics, Lake Champlain, and the Adirondacks. Eastward are the White Mountains, while Mount Ascutney is the only prominent peak to the southeast.

When ready, return to your car via the same trail.

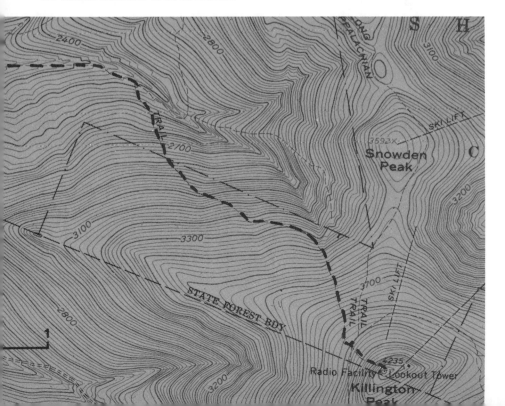

Deer Leap Mountain

Class: II & V
Distance (round trip): 2.7 miles
Hiking time: 2 hours
Vertical rise: 680 feet
USGS 7.5' Pico Peak

This climb could be viewed as two separate hikes. The loop you'll make will bring you to Deer Leap Mountain's two peaks and across its saddle over vastly different routes. The ascent via the Long Trail and Deer Leap Trail is gradual; the descent from Little Deer Leap (the southern peak) drops a precipitous 450 feet in just .3 mile! You'll use your hands often as you pick your way down over steep-ledged and badly washed out sections. Plan to retrace your steps and avoid this last .3 mile if traveling with small children or if you are unsure of yourself.

Start at the Long Trail North in Sherburne Pass. At the height-of-land on US 4 between Rutland and Sherburne you will see the Inn at Long Trail. Just to the east a sign marks the Long and Appalachian trails. There is off-the-road parking on both sides of the highway here.

Climb 150 feet from the road to the fork where the Deer Leap and Long trails split. You are taking the gradual way up and the steeper way down. Keep right on the white-blazed Long Trail.

The trail winds along the mountainside. Above and to the left hundreds of large boulders crowd the slope. The path is also littered with rocks and small boulders, so walk carefully. Below to the right US 4 parallels your route. The loud motor vehicle noises remind you that you haven't yet escaped civilization.

The trail swings upward to the left and begins to slice along the east side of the slope. Huge masses of ledge jut out from the hillside above, and eventually the path comes up to meet them. Pass upward through a slender opening between these giants. Roots and stones continue to make the walking rough as you climb the moderate grade. Then, as you meander over short dips and rises, the slope becomes more gradual and the footing smoother.

After roughly .5 mile the woods suddenly open before you. The sloping hillsides disappear and you enter a flat clearing. Many signs mark this important trail intersection. This is the junction of the Appalachian and Long trails. From here the Long Trail continues north to Canada, while the Appalachian swings east toward New Hampshire and its northern terminus on Mount Katahdin in Maine. Keep left on the Long Trail.

The path remains flat except for occasional bends around boulders. Becoming strewn with rocks, it swings gradually up to the left. It passes a huge moss-covered boulder supporting an old birch tree. Roots cling to the stone surface like octopus tentacles.

Thin, fragile-looking trees line the trail as it begins a very gradual, long, winding descent. At 1.2 miles the Deer Leap and Long trails rejoin. Follow the blue-blazed Deer Leap Trail as it turns sharply left.

Short spruces take over the left hillside as the trail passes briefly through a steeper section. The grade becomes more gradual as you wind through more young spruces, and then more moderate, and finally steep, before returning to its familiar gradual incline.

Some of the large tree trunks and stumps that line the way have hundreds of small, evenly spaced holes girdling their bark. They were made by the yellow-bellied sapsucker. This bird makes the holes while eating the inner bark. He wisely returns later to eat both the sap and the insects that have been attracted to it.

Thick stands of spruce gather around the trail just before it passes through an area dense with ferns. Two large trees next to a huge boulder on the right mark a lookoff. Limited views to the northwest are available here.

The path winds upward and becomes steeper. It flattens out in an open area edged by ledge on the left. Passing through thick spruces, the path becomes spongy with needles. You soon reach a sign titled Deer Leap Height (just west of Big Deer Leap, the northern peak of Deer Leap Mountain). The elevation here is 2,770 feet.

The trail drops first moderately, then gradually, into the valley separating Deer Leap Mountain's two peaks. At 2.2 miles you come to a sign indicating it is about .5 mile to Sherburne Pass.

Cross a small brook and climb steeply through white birches and under overhanging ledge. Walk along the ridge

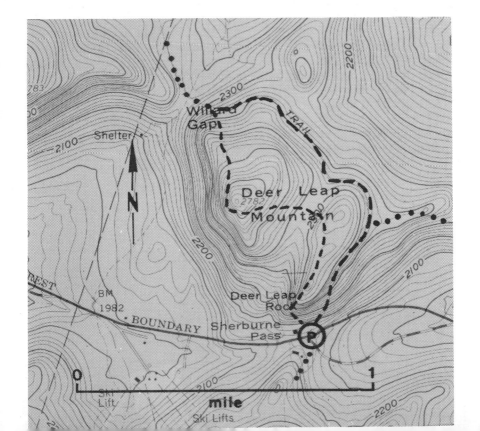

Lower lookout on Deer Leap Mountain

to the sign for Little Deer Leap, the southern peak. The elevation here is 2,580 feet.

The path twists and turns through a spruce-lined area. Traffic sounds get louder as you begin to descend. Soon you reach a huge mass of white, quartz-streaked ledge. This is the Upper Lookout. Climb up for striking views of Sherburne Pass and surrounding mountains. One hundred feet below, you walk out onto the Lower Lookout. From this ledge you look up to Pico Peak across Sherburne Pass and down to US 4.

The remaining descent to your car is very steep and slippery. You slide down over smooth ledge and through jumbled sections of massive boulders. After stepping down a log ladder and using a nylon cable along a particularly steep section, you drop quickly to US 4 and your car. If traveling with small children, or in bad weather, or if the drop just looks too steep, don't hesitate to retrace your steps from the lower lookout back to your starting point.

Blue Ridge Mountain

Class: III
Distance (round trip): 4.8 miles
Hiking time: 2 1/2 hours
Vertical rise: 1,487 feet
USGS 7.5' Chittenden

A beautiful, cascading waterfall and hordes of yellow birches enrich the sides of the 2.4-mile-long Canty Trail up the south side of Blue Ridge Mountain. It takes you to the mountain's summit after a steep ascent through deciduous forests and a final meandering walk through evergreens. Once there, you get one of the best close views of the Coolidge Range. You can also look to the west beyond Rutland to Bird and Herrick mountains with the Adirondacks on the horizon. On a clear day, when the light is right, you can see what appears to be a misty field just in front of the Adirondacks. This, of course, is Lake Champlain. Stratton and Dorset mountains lie to the south and southwest.

To reach the trail's start, drive east on US 4 for 6.2 miles from the junction of US 4 and US 7 in Rutland. Turn north onto Old Turnpike Road (the sign reads simply "Turnpike Road"). Drive .6 mile and turn left onto the second dirt road where there is an arrowed sign to the Tall Timber Camping Area (a private campground). There are also trail signs for "Blue Ridge." Bear left at the fork and continue until you come to the large

main building. Park your car in the field to the left.

Following the road, walk to the right beyond this large brown building. Continue right at the fork here. You will quickly come to a number of signs. An arrow points the way to Blue Ridge. The trail you want is marked with tin can tops painted blue.

Turn left into the woods and follow the blue blazes, which are initially paired with the green ones of the shorter Green Trail. A trail junction soon appears. Your route leaves the Green Trail, crosses the brook, and bears right. Very soon, you ford the brook again and resume a gradual walk.

The sides of the path are thickly forested with evergreens. After paralleling the brook, you cross it once more at .3 mile, this time with the help of a log bridge. There is still no noticeable gain in elevation as the path proceeds over a series of dips and rises. After crossing still another stream, you follow an old road for a short distance.

There is one more stream to cross at .6 mile before the trail begins the more serious climb toward the summit. As-

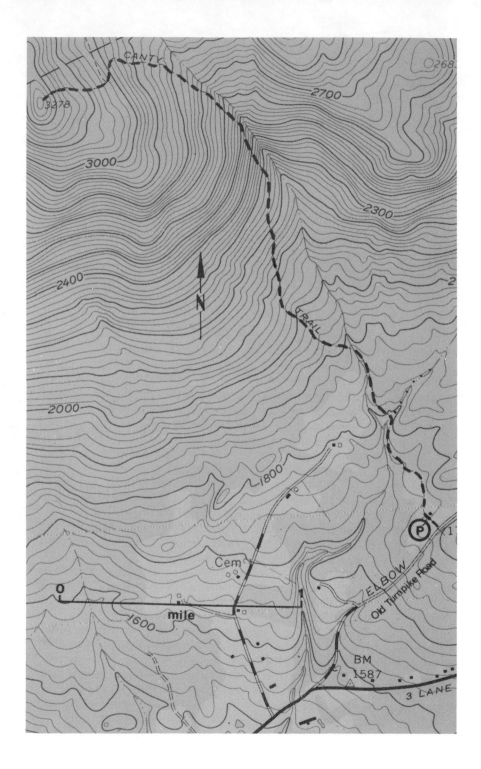

cend the steep stream bank and follow the winding path. It turns right onto another old road that parallels the brook below to the right.

The trail soon becomes more jumbled with rocks as the slope increases sharply. This is the steepest and most rugged section of the entire trail. Closer to the summit the path resumes its gradual, meandering ways.

There are large-tooth aspen along the pathside here. These northeastern trees resemble the trembling aspen somewhat, but have heavier twigs and larger, coarser leaves. The round-toothed, heart-shaped leaves are their most distinctive characteristic. The soft, light wood is used for pulp, excelsior, boxes, and matches.

After approximately 1.5 miles, you can hear rushing water below to the right. You might want to make your way down through the woods for a closer look. The cascading white water slides over smooth ledge and narrows to slither around rock outcroppings. It swirls into tranquil pools before tumbling downward again.

Paralleling the water, the path follows an old washed-out road. The higher sides offer more solid footing than the rutted, rocky middle. Yellow birches have been the most prominent tree along the way. These trees display silver-yellow bark and may grow as high as one hundred feet. Their double-toothed oval leaves have a wintergreen fragrance. Stands of these trees are a sign of rich, well-drained soil.

Continuing upward, the path becomes much more gradual. Shining club moss gathers its glossy spires to form sparkling green patches at the base of tree trunks. Evergreen spills cushion your walking as the trail brushes between spruces and balsams. The deliciously pungent fragrance of balsam fills your nostrils.

Cascade

After meandering upward to the left, the path suddenly swings right at 2.3 miles. Scramble over some ledge and enter the clearing at the summit. Above to the right are large rocks that serve as vantage points. They will enable you to see in all possible directions.

Return to your car by the same route.

Mount Carmel

Class: III
Distance (round trip): 3.6 miles
Hiking time: 2 1/2 hours
Vertical rise: 1,598 feet
USGS 7.5' Chittenden; USGS 7.5' Mount Carmel

The hike to the summit of Mount Carmel is a good one to save for an overcast day. The views from the top are limited in any event (the tower that used to offer a glorious panorama is down), and the forest is sufficiently varied to be of interest.

The first part of this hike follows the New Boston Trail. To reach its beginning, drive north on Mountain Top Road from the military memorial statue in the town of Chittenden. After 1.7 miles bear right onto Forest Road number 99, at the fork just beyond the Mountain Top Inn. After approximately 2 miles, you will come to a large cleared area near a tubular steel gate. The New Boston Trail begins here.

For the first mile, the blue blazes of this path follow a jeep trail. On both sides of the trail, rotting oak and beech stumps display bracketed growths of artist's fungus (so named for the pictures craftsmen like to paint on their smooth white undersides). Shades of brown and tan color the smoothly rippled sections of their upper surfaces. Much of this section is a pleasant walk, with only slight increases in elevation.

The red blazes of the Mount Carmel State Forest cross the path at 1 mile. Just beyond at the end of the jeep trail is the David Logan Shelter, used by hikers on the Long Trail, which is just ahead. A spring bubbles a bit north on the New Boston Trail.

Follow the winding, blue-blazed footpath to the left of the shelter. The packed-dirt path swings upward to the right and reaches the Long Trail at 1.3 miles.

Turn left onto the Long Trail and follow its white blazes north. Climbing steadily you arrive at the Mount Carmel Trail at 1.9 miles. Go right onto this trail. Look carefully as it is unblazed, not a well-trodden path, and unmaintained. It may be difficult for the average hiker to locate.

The way swings around to the left through bunches of hobblebush. Its leaves are large (four-to-eight inches), nearly round, finely toothed, and heart-shaped at the base. In winter, distinctive buds will help you recognize this shrub: two small leaves enclose a tiny flower at the twig ends. These twigs and buds are favored by deer for winter browsing.

The path twists and turns up Mount Carmel's south slope. You really have to lean into this steep ascent. After entering a small clearing covered with spruce and balsam spills, the way climbs straight up to the summit.

The Lookout Tower was dismantled years ago, but by climbing some short spruce or balsam trees you can view Bloodroot Mountain to the north-northwest (3,485 feet); Round Mountain to the north-northeast (3,342 feet); and Mount Nickawaket almost due west (2,753 feet). Follow the same route back to your car.

31

Abbey Pond

Class: II
Distance (round trip): 4.6 miles
Hiking time: 2 1/4 hours
Vertical rise: 1,250 feet
USGS 7.5' South Mountain

You will be touched by Abbey Pond's primitiveness and tranquility. An early morning or late afternoon visit to the pond might acquaint you with some of its more bashful neighbors. The masked nocturnal raccoon may leave his long-fingered pawprints after feeding on frogs and crayfish. Deer come to drink and browse on pondside shrubbery. Muskrats nest along the sides of the pond and sometimes build above-water homes like those of the beaver.

Drive north on US 7 into Middlebury. Pass the Addison County Court House and take the next right. At the stop sign bear right onto Seminary Street Extension. Bear left at the fork after 1.4 miles onto Quarry Road. Follow it to the end where it meets VT 116 (Case Street) and turn left (north). After another .7 mile you'll spot a sign for the Abbey Pond Trail on the east side of the road. Turn east onto the dirt road, which divides immediately. Take the right fork and follow the dark blue blazes on the trees.

Approximately .4 mile after turning onto the dirt road you'll reach an intersection. Straight ahead, blue blazes mark the start of the trail. Pull your car well

off the road to avoid interfering with gravel trucks.

Follow the blue blazes along an old logging road. The track is wide and gradual. Some rocks intrude but are easily avoided. Then giant glacial boulders, many with trees and mosses flourishing atop their great masses, appear to the right.

The pitch increases. Swinging left, the dirt path passes below moss-covered ledge. After approximately .2 mile, you cross over fast-flowing Muddy Brook, which finds its source in Abbey Pond. The bridge here is badly rotted, so cross the brook carefully. The Forest Service plans to rebuild it in the near future. To the right a twenty-five-foot waterfall spills into a series of small pools.

Soon the trail swings right and begins to parallel the brook, whose muffled rushing will accompany you for some time. At .6 mile the brook again passes beneath the trail. Bearing left, the path maintains a steady upward incline. The brook courses along the bottom of the ravine below.

At 1.1 miles, on a more gentle incline, the trail passes over a black boggy area and crosses a gentler section of the brook via narrow logs. Beyond the brook the path wanders over and around small rocks. It remains flat, with only minimal dips and rises, the rest of the way to the pond. The ground may be a bit spongy underfoot.

You come out of the thick woods, and arrive at Abbey Pond. Two small peaks rise above and are reflected in its waters. Looking around the pond you'll see a beaver dam at the near end. Look down the pond to the dead trees rising at the other end and you'll see the lodge itself.

Sit quietly on a sun-warmed rock near the water's edge; watch and listen. A salamander may be scuttling along the

bottom. These tailed amphibians eat insects, worms, and other small invertebrates. In early summer, their eggs are found in jellylike clusters in the shallows.

The pond is a haven for ducks and geese. Abbey Pond's shallowness and its aquatic plants attract the surface-feeding ducks such as mallards and blacks. You may see them "tipping up" as they eat off the lush bottom.

The belted kingfisher also lives here.

He has distinctive blue-grey markings, a white throat band, a large bill, and a crested head. He flies erratically yet can hover suspended over the water before plunging in for small fish.

The trout, too, find Abbey Pond beautiful. Creating circles of ripples as they surface for food, they often leap completely out of the water in their pursuit of insects.

Return to your car filled with some of the quiet of this woodland pond.

Abbey Pond

Mount Abraham

Class: III
Distance (round trip): 5 miles
Hiking time: 3 1/2 hours
Vertical rise: 1,642 feet
USGS 7.5' Lincoln

Mount Abraham is among the more popular climbs for day hikers, as well as a favorite with backpackers walking the Long Trail. Its easy access and striking views—it has one of the most far-reaching panoramas on the entire Long Trail—make it a very desirable destination.

Early settlers called Mount Abraham "Potatoe Hill" because of its resemblance to an oversized, well-banked potato mound. This name was not completely accepted, however, and map publishers changed it to Lincoln Mountain—for the Revolutionary War figure General Benjamin Lincoln. When Colonel Joseph Battell bought the mountain in the late 1800s (as part of his plan for conserving Vermont forests), he renamed it Mount Abraham, after our sixteenth president. He then named the neighboring mountain to the north Lincoln Peak.

To reach the stretch of the Long Trail that climbs Mount Abraham (maintained by the U.S. Forest Service), travel along the Lincoln-Warren Highway from either Lincoln or Warren to the top of the Lincoln Gap. There is ample parking just below the crest, on the Warren side, both off and along the road. However, on a

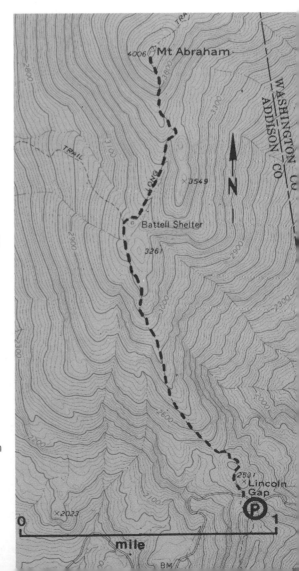

clear weekend you might arrive to find the roadside already packed with vehicles of all kinds.

Walk up the road, toward Lincoln, to the height-of-land, where you will find the trail ascending a short, steep embankment on the north side of the highway. At the top of the embankment the trail forks. Stay to the left. The path narrows as it passes behind slender young birches. White blazes guide you right and gradually upward. Surprisingly, there are a number of abrupt descents during the first half of your trek up Mount Abraham. The trail swings sharply left, then right, as it drops down over rooted steps. Dipping steadily, it switches back sharply right and winds past a long series of moss-covered ledges.

Then the smoothness of the path yields to rocks as you pass upward through snowy birches. A small section of ledge insures a gradual rise. Once on top you gaze down a short, steep dropoff. Serpentine roots cling to the ledge, providing sure footing. Moving gradually upward, you come to red blazes flanking and crossing the trail.

These mark the boundary of the Green Mountain National Forest.

Two huge boulders squeeze the trail at the 1.2-mile mark. (They are called "the Carpenters" after two trail workers so named.) Old stumps, rotted into a variety of poses, dot the way.

The 2,410-foot base elevation at Lincoln Gap is responsible for the fact that the highway through it is closed in winter, and for the lack of traditional hardwood forests along this trail. Instead, the trail-sides teem with fluffy young spruce and balsam. They are so closely packed that you wonder how they will survive. Stately older trees rise above these younger ones.

An opening in the thick trees suddenly appears. Straight ahead you can see the massive dome of Mount Abraham. Tree-covered except for the actual summit, it appears quite imposing from this distance. You are now roughly 1 mile from the top.

A trickling brook crosses the trail. It offers cool, refreshing water and a good excuse to rest. Just ahead, the Battell Trail joins from the left. Battell Shelter is

Nearing Mount Abraham's summit

250 yards upward to the right. A sturdy, smooth-sided structure, it can sleep six to eight hikers. Spring water is available 100 feet to the east.

From the shelter take the main trail to the left. Thick stands of spruce and balsam create a cloistered atmosphere. Twists and turns over intermittent stretches of ledge necessitate careful stepping. Approaching the summit amid dwarfed scrub growth, the trail confronts an unusually beautiful boulder. White but veined with black, the giant piece of quartz is surely a rarity. Against the drab grey-greens of the ledge and spruce, it stands out strikingly.

Reaching the summit, you see several circles of piled rocks. Looking like the bottom of unfinished stone igloos, these barriers offer protection from blustery winds. If you look closely on the ground, you will find the surveyor's disk with the words "Potatoe Hill" on it.

The views are superb. You can look west across Lake Champlain and clearly see the Adirondacks, with Mount Marcy most prominent. Southward, Green Mountain peaks stretch as far as Killington. Mount Ascutney looms on the horizon to the southeast. Mounts Lafayette and Washington are in the distant east. Looking north, you can follow a panoramic profile from the distinctive Camel's Hump, past Mount Mansfield, north to Jay Peak and Belvidere Mountain.

The Warren-Sugarbush Airport (a local center for soaring enthusiasts) is below and to the east. You can become mesmerized by the gliders if you're on Mount Abraham when the weather is clear and the winds are right.

Return to reality; your transportation awaits 2.5 miles below at Lincoln Gap.

Mount Ellen

Class: III
Distance (round trip): 9.7 miles
Hiking time: 6 1/2 - 7 hours
Vertical rise: 2,508 feet
USGS 7.5' Mount Ellen

Although Mount Ellen's wooded summit is the ultimate destination on this challenging hike, the best views are from just below the peak. The ascent itself is steep, rugged, and continuous.

Mount Ellen shares with Camel's Hump the honor of being Vermont's third highest peak. Only Killington and Mansfield rise higher. This mountain is not as close to access roads as the others, however, so the trails to its summit are longer. The climb—although gradual at times—is steady and has you leaning into the slope almost all the way. Prepare for a long day's hiking.

From the junction of VT 17 and VT 116 northeast of Bristol, go east on VT 17. Follow it 3.2 miles to the signed road leading to Jerusalem. Go right at the store and travel 1.2 miles to the wooden signpost with a small worn sign for the Jerusalem Trail, on the corner of a road leading left. Follow the road for .7 mile to the start of the Jerusalem Trail. Park off the road to the right in a pull over. Follow the blue blazes into the woods and across a stream to the right.

Long, straight stretches, steady in-clines, and slim trees characterize the surroundings over much of the first mile. At .8 mile, the path swings left and begins its steepest climb so far. A blue-blazed boulder, entrenched in the middle of the trail, marks the spot.

Thick stands of maples fill the forest as the grade maintains its upward trend. Both black and sugar maples grow here. (Black maple sap is also used to produce the famous Vermont maple syrup.) These two types of maples are distinguishable by their leaves. The black maple's are three-lobed with shallow notches and drooping edges. The sugar maple's are five-lobed with moderately deep notches and firm edges.

The trail bears right after 1.2 miles and changes direction from east to south. The high ridgeline of the Green Mountain chain now becomes visible above and to the left.

Dense thickets of hobblebush edge the path as it narrows and steepens. This straggly shrub is common throughout northern New England. The clustered five-petaled white flowers appear in May and June. The fruit (nonpoisonous but acidic) begins to develop in August and changes from red to black at maturity.

The trail climbs a short, steep slope before weaving between stands of thin white birches. An old grassy road joins from the right at 1.7 miles. The way becomes refreshingly gradual in places, crosses two brooks, and then resumes its steep climb.

The easy walking has ended. For the next .5 mile the trail is very steep and rocks, ledge, and roots make the climbing more difficult.

At 2.3 miles the Jerusalem and Long trails meet. From here it is 1.8 miles to the summit of Mount Ellen. Turn right onto the Long Trail South. This section is quite typical of the Long Trail as it winds along ridges of the Green Mountains. It dips and rises while crossing from one side of the ridge line to the other. The footing ranges from rocky and rooty to boggy.

The rough trail descends gradually into a gully. Rising out, it passes through an area covered with many shades of green growth. Moss begins around tree trunks above the path and sweeps down over vertical ledge faces to the edge of the trail itself. Tree-filtered sunbeams highlight the rainbow of greenery.

Mount Ellen can be seen rising ahead as you continue through a lush, damp area. Rocks and dead logs are choked by a variety of plant life. Wood sorrel, wavy broom moss, and blister and reindeer lichen exist side by side.

At 3.1 miles the path climbs right over rocks and roots and begins a steady ascent to the summit. Dampness makes the trail slippery in spots.

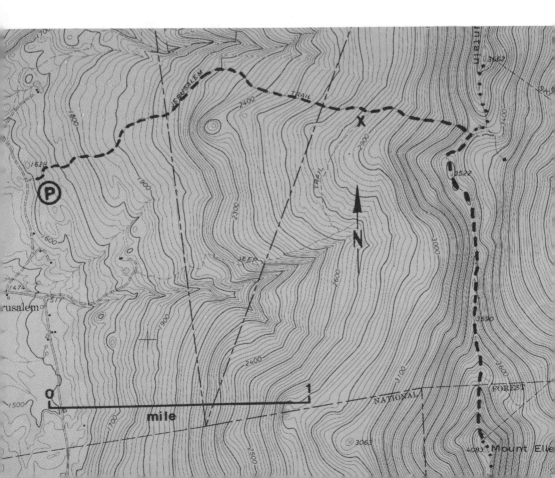

Trail to Mount Ellen

The Long Trail bears to the right and climbs through dense balsam firs below and to the west of a ski slope. The trail then enters the ski slope, and turns to the right, passing the upper station of the Sugarbush North chairlift. Look back down the slope for a view north to Camel's Hump and Mount Mansfield. Mount Alice, and Bald and Scrag mountains are to the northeast. To the southeast you can pick out the peaks of Mount Cushman, Mount Olympus, and Rochester Mountain. New Hampshire summits form the distant backdrop.

Follow the white blazes past the end of the chairlift and up the short slope to the wooded summit. Find a spot in the sun to warm yourself and rest in preparation for the return trip.

34

Scrag Mountain

Class: III
Distance (round trip): 3.7 miles
Hiking time: 3 hours
Vertical rise: 1,491 feet
USGS 7.5' Waitsfield

The most beautiful white birch forests we've seen can be found in the cool woods on the slopes of Scrag Mountain.

To climb the trail through these handsome trees, drive to Waitsfield on VT 100. Turn southeast off VT 100 at the Jilson Public Library (the yellow brick building). Drive .4 mile, through a covered bridge, to a fork in the road. Follow the road to the left over a narrow bridge and up a steep hill for about .7 mile. Turn right onto a gravel road named Cross Road, which comes into a four-way intersection after .7 mile. Go straight across and continue for another 1.1 miles. The road will become rougher and runs parallel to a stone wall. At the top of a hill you will see a drive to the right; continue downhill .2 mile to a road fork. Take the right fork, and go uphill .3 mile. Park by an old apple tree marking the remains of a stone foundation. The road to the left of the parking lot is the trail. Logging has taken place at the trailhead recently, making it difficult to locate, but the trailhead is marked.

At .1 mile you will come to a large hemlock marking a fork. Take the Scrag Trail to the left. The trail angles through dense patches of ferns and into thicker woods. It is still a crude road at this point, quite bumpy and rocky.

A few minutes of walking brings you to a clear stream. This is the last certain water on the trail to the summit. Pause here to refresh and prepare yourself for the climb ahead. After the stream, the trail scrambles up over rocks, roots, and boulders. Young maples and beeches crowd the way. Though not excessively steep, the pitch of the upward grade is continually challenging.

An especially interesting large rock obstructs this lower part of the trail. Its surface is colored several shades of brown and pocketed with rounded depressions. Furry moss softens its face.

Scattered, solitary trees herald your approach to the promised assembly of white birches. They'll light your way for one-third of the hike to the summit. Pick your way across dried stream beds, by a decaying three-log bridge across a small gully, and then around the numerous rocks that have spilled down the trail. As you climb higher, spruces join, and finally replace, the white birches.

After 1.3 miles of hiking, the trail divides. A sign indicates that the short trail straight ahead will lead to water at the first stream or the second well. However, it is better to carry your own drinking water to the top, as this supply is doubtful. Another sign points left toward Scrag Trail. Follow this left switchback .3 mile to the summit.

As you move along this section of the trail, look through the trees to the left for a glimpse of blue mountain silhouettes. The path winds over alternately rising and level areas as it swings widely right. Climb past a brown cabin into a small clearing. Limited views of various mountains, including the Lincoln Range, may be enjoyed from here.

For an opportunity to experience an extended circle of mountain views, continue along the trail to the top of Scrag Mountain (2,911 feet), where there used to be a fire lookout tower. Only four small pillars from the foundation remain. You'll climb over ledge on this last stretch of trail.

Camel's Hump and Mount Mansfield figure more prominently along the northwestern horizon. The Lincoln Range lines the west; south to north its peaks are: Mount Abraham, Lincoln Peak, Nancy Hanks Peak, Cutts Peak, and Mount Ellen. To the southwest you'll see the Presidential Range (not to be confused with the similarly named range in New Hampshire). Looking east you have: Butterfield, Spruce, and Signal mountains. Mount Hunger, Mount Worcester, and White Rock Mountain are to the north.

When ready, return by the same route.

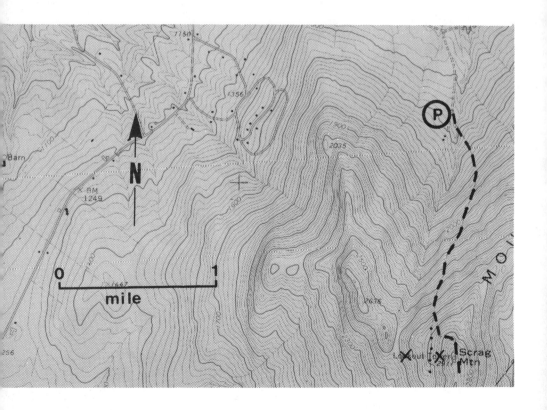

35

Spruce Mountain

Class: III
Distance (round trip): 3.9 miles
Hiking time: 3 hours
Vertical rise: 1,177 feet
USGS 15' Plainfield; USGS 15' East Barre

Spruce Mountain lets you "get back to nature" in the purest sense. No summit roads or other encroachments of modern man scar its slopes. Its nearly twenty-five hundred-acres comprise one of the most remote mountain tracts remaining in the entire state.

The land also contains one of Vermont's best wildlife habitats. Black bear breed here, as do numerous other woodland creatures. One Spruce Mountain ornithological study a few years ago recorded sightings of seventy different kinds of birds.

The natural balance of Spruce Mountain has not yet been disturbed. But many of Vermont's unspoiled areas have been disappearing rapidly: sold to builders, developers, and speculators who care more for money than for the land. If we are to enjoy the peace, quiet, and exhilaration of communing with nature, this area—and others like it—must remain "wild."

The road to Spruce Mountain is located 4.5 miles south of Plainfield. Take the road leading south off Route 2 in Plainfield and from this junction go through town about .5 mile to a fork. Go right onto East Hill Road and follow it 4 miles. Do not take the road to the left after crossing a small bridge. Take the next left and, after cresting two hills, take another left onto Spruce Mountain Rd.

This road eventually swings left, with a narrow offshoot going right. Keep left here. Becoming very rocky and rutted, the road leads to an iron swing gate where there is ample parking on both sides. Should you be unable to reach this point by car, park at any of the widened areas along the way and walk the short distance to the gate. The red blazes to the right and left of the barrier mark the boundary of Jones State Forest.

The trail bears right from the gate. The initial section of the trail is a wide smooth road. Follow the fork to the left, and after .5 mile, take the trail which passes to the left of the large hemlock. As it crests a small knoll and begins heading downward, you can see the abandoned Spruce Mountain fire tower high in the distance to the left.

The way becomes increasingly grassy as it leads upward. The mountain's outline is occasionally visible through trees to the left as the road continues its gradual climb. When you swing left and enter dense woods, the grassy path fills with stones. Several damp, muddied patches lie ahead.

Cross-country ski trails have been cut through these woods and crisscross the main hiking trail ahead. They are marked with orange blazes. When you have a choice of paths to take, stay with the older trail. If you are uncertain, remember that the ski trails were cut because the main trail is too steep for skiers to use, but it is fine for hikers.

Making your way up this section of trail, stepping gingerly from rock to rock, you come to a log bridge across a slow-moving brook. Beyond it the trail widens somewhat and becomes softer underfoot—although rocks continue to speckle the way. Walking is slower as you negotiate the bumpy footing.

Veering left, the path climbs moderately. Spruce and balsam line the trail as it continues to steepen. You approach two huge, looming glacial boulders at the 1.3-mile mark. Short spruces grow atop them and appear to be anchored by only a thick carpet of moss. The trail swings left in front of these gargantuan guards and begins a passage over sloping ledge.

Scraggy old spruces and balsams stand watch over smaller, bushy ones as the trail climbs more steeply. It seems impossible that the closely bunched young trees can find room to grow. The path passes over long sections of beautiful white-with-black-flecks granite

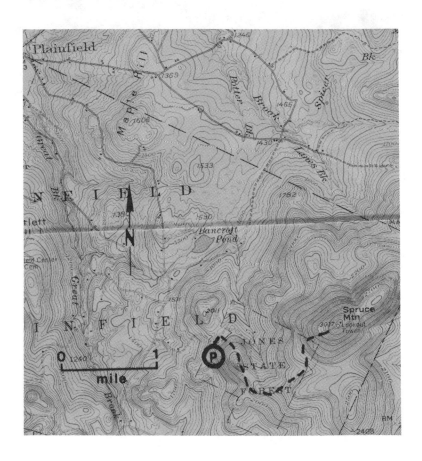

View of Spruce Mountain

ledge as it winds upward to the right. Then roots slither across the trail as it begins its final push to the top. The way suddenly levels out, becoming a dirt path lined with grass and ferns. The abbreviated height of the trees, combined with the low grass and shrubs at the trail sides, creates an open, airy atmosphere.

The old fire tower can be seen ahead, as you pass more slabs of granite. Both it and the small cabin just beyond, where the fire warden lived from April through October, are deserted and show signs of lack of maintenance. Planes now virtually monopolize surveillance duties in Vermont.

The views here are truly spectacular. On a clear day you can see west across Lake Champlain to the Adirondack peaks eighty miles away. Mount Washington's summit is visible seventy-five miles to the east. Numerous Vermont peaks can be seen within these perimeters.

Return to your car by the same route.

36

Osmore Pond and Little Deer Mountain

Class: II
Distance (round trip): 5.8 miles
Hiking time: 3 1/2 hours
Vertical rise: 660 feet
USGS 15' Plainfield

More than twenty thousand acres of land lie within the boundaries of Groton State Forest, making it the largest single unit of state-owned land in Vermont. Numerous game animals, especially deer, thrive here. Groton's spruce-fir swamps are a prime area for winter deer yarding.

People come to Groton State Forest for many reasons: they picnic, swim, camp, cook, hunt, go fishing and boating, enjoy the scenery, mob the refreshment stand, and, of course, go hiking. The trails marked with blue paint are for hikers and snowshoers only; those marked with orange reflecting diamonds are "multi-purpose" (all-terrain vehicles excluded). One hike here we like takes in both Osmore Pond and Little Deer Mountain. The walk to the pond is pleasantly undemanding; the hike up Little Deer, moderately strenuous. A lot of logging takes place in the Groton State Forest area, which affects trail locations. Hikers should check with forest personnel for current trail conditions before taking this hike.

Groton State Forest is located on the road that connects US 302 west of Groton and US 2 east of Marshfield. Drive from either end to the green and

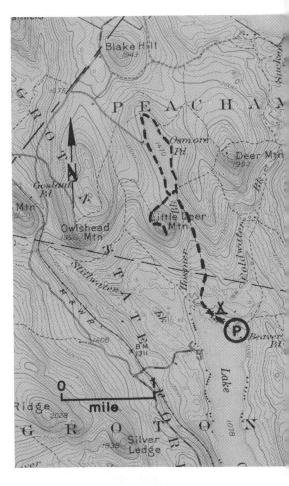

yellow sign for Groton State Forest listing Big Deer, Stillwater, and Lake Groton. Turn in here and follow the forest road for 1.6 miles to the parking lot and nature center building, the first left past the Big Deer Campgrounds. Detailed trail maps are available at the Nature Center, and a State Park Naturalist is in residence during the summer and fall.

Walk back along the same road for .3 mile. On the right you will see brown and white signs for Osmore Pond and New Discovery. The path you are looking for starts into the woods just to the right of the signs. The blue blazes mark this as a trail for hikers only.

Sides of the trail overflow with fern growth. This gives the open woods a softly feathered look that accents the startling whiteness of paper birches and the shiny creaminess of yellow birches. The trail parallels a merrily flowing brook, occasionally dipping down near it. Where you begin to climb gradually the path swings away from the brook. Moving through the shadows of a stand of spruce, you can hear the wind brush the tree tops. Behind and below, the brook sound is soft and gushing.

At 1.2 miles you reach a small clearing where several trail signs are posted.

A brown and white one points straight ahead for the Osmore Pond Hiking Loop. Heading in the direction the sign points, you shortly are able to see the waters of Osmore Pond. The loop trail winds gently around the edge of this lovely isolated pond. On the eastern side it parallels the shore about fifty feet in, but two foot-paths lead to clear views at the water's edge. Rising above the southwestern end is Little Deer Mountain.

The sturdy log structures you pass are some of the more than twenty-five group camping lean-tos in the state forest. They may be used for wilderness camping according to the forest rules. In addition, state personnel maintain 225 individual camping sites.

You pass through occasional spruce bogs as you make your way around the pond. At the northern tip, the trail veers away from the water. You pick your way over another boggy area and a small streamlet. Continuing along the western shore, the path closely follows the pond's edge. Watch carefully for the blue-blazed markers as short young spruces and heavy side growth struggle to hide the trail. On this side you will also find a rustic picnic area with water and facilities.

View across Osmore Pond to Little Deer Mountain

From here you also have a clear view of Big Deer Mountain rising above the eastern shore of Osmore Pond. Nearby, sun-bleached logs poke their bulk above the water's surface. If you quietly approach one of these logs on a warm sunny day you may see pond sliders or other turtles basking in the sun.

Near the southern end of the pond, the trail winds gradually to the right, and power lines appear overhead. The path swings sharply left to a multi-signed trail junction.

Signs point straight ahead to Lake Groton, Peacham Pond, and Big Deer Mountain. Turn right here and follow the path beneath the power lines. After approximately 100 yards you will come to a sign pointing the way to Little Deer Mountain. It is .4 mile to the summit from here.

Go right on the blue-blazed path, which maintains a moderate pitch up the mountain. After a short distance, it makes a ninety-degree turn to the left. Watch carefully for the blue blazes at this point. The trail remains smooth and very enjoyable as it continues its moderate climb.

Near the summit the path swings left and leads into a small cleared area. There are limited views of nearby hills and an open look down the length of Lake Groton. To the southwest is Spruce Mountain, its high, pointed peak topped by an abandoned fire tower.

Hike back down the same trail to the sign for Little Deer Mountain. Go left onto the path beneath the power lines and back to the signed intersection. Go right toward Lake Groton, Big Deer Mountain, and Peacham Pond.

Bearing left, the path crosses a wood bridge. The brook beneath is the outlet of Osmore Pond. This is the start of the gurgling brook that parallels the stretch of trail you first walked.

A series of log planks have been placed on the trail to aid your passage over a final boggy area. Shortly after crossing this wet section you return to the junction of the Osmore Pond Hiking Loop, Big Deer Mountain Trail, and the trail to Lake Groton. You have now hiked 4 miles and have 1.2 miles left on the trail toward Lake Groton and the forest road and then .3 mile to the nature center parking lot.

37

Big Deer Mountain

Class II
Distance (round trip): 4.6 miles
Hiking time: 3 hours
Vertical rise: 912 feet
USGS 15' Plainfield

This hike offers you another nice way to spend your time in Groton State Forest (see Hike 36). Some entrances to trails are closed after Labor Day, but the one described here remains open. Be aware that there is continued logging in Groton State Forest, which may affect the trail system. Hikers should check with forest personnel for curent trail conditions.

Because the trail up Big Deer Mountain is both pretty and gentle all along its 2.3-mile length, it does not depend upon spectacular views for its charm. The flat, rolling path would be an ideal foliage walk in the fall. Maples, elms, and birches surround the occasional balsams and spruces. An openness along the trailsides inspires a sense of freedom and offers deep views into the woods.

The starting point for this hike is located in the parking lot for the nature center at Groton State Forest. To reach it, drive along the road between US 302 west of Groton and US 2 east of Marshfield and turn in by the state forest sign for Lake Groton, Stillwater, and Big Deer Mountain. Follow the forest road 1.6 miles, past the Big Deer Campgrounds, to the nature center.

Walk to the far right-hand corner of the parking lot and pick up the Martins

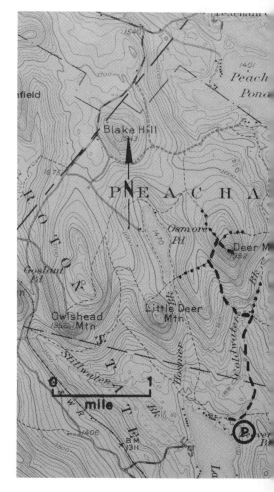

Coldwater Brook

Pond Road-Peacham Bog Trail. In .5 mile you will find a sign for Coldwater Brook Trail. Turn left and stay on this trail for the rest of the hike.

The path slithers around large rocks and passes through clusters of sparkling white birches as the hillside begins to slope steeply down to the right. The waters of Coldwater Brook can occasionally be seen and heard below. Rolling along over slight dips and rises, the trail veers left past a large triangular boulder. You cross several black muddy patches and then pass through stands of closely bunched spruces and balsams before re-entering the young hardwood forest.

Take time to observe the various kinds of greenery all around. Lady fern and pinulose woodfern swarm around hobblebush and striped maple. Close to the ground you can see shining club moss, bunchberries, and ground pine.

After passing two large glacial boulders guarding the sloping fields of fern to the left, the way narrows and becomes crisscrossed with roots. The trail swings right, and the hillside to the left draws closer. A gentle brook tumbles across the path at approximately .9 mile. Water caresses the many round mossy stones herded between its edges. Beyond the brook the trail swings sharply left before winding right toward Coldwater Brook.

The roar of gushing water draws your

attention. Stop here for a delightful, shady respite. The brook's flowing softness turns frenzied as it rushes through a wide rocky chute. White water and foam gush into a quieter pool below. An archway in the wall of huge stones flanking the brook allows some water to flow to the edge, but most continues over a low dam into the placid pool.

Continuing up a moderate incline, you approach a fork in the trail. The Coldwater Brook Trail continues left here toward Osmore Pond. If you turn right you will cross the brook and within a few hundred yards find a winterized shelter. Retrace your steps and continue on the trail to Osmore Pond. It passes through light woods before crossing one of Coldwater Brook's small tributaries, which it then parallels awhile. Recrossing the brook, the trail begins a moderate climb to the right. Glacial boulders protrude from the open woods as it becomes

rockier. The path leads over the rounded stones of an old stream bed before returning to its flat, packed-dirt ways.

At 1.9 miles you enter a clearing with many signs. Follow the one to Big Deer Mountain up to the right. Climbing more steeply, you pass through expansive stands of white and then yellow birch. At 2.1 miles another sign points you sharply right. You are approximately .2 mile from the summit. Climbing through slender birches and over and around boulders, the trail becomes progressively steeper. Its edges are dotted with reindeer lichen, whose tiny antlered design makes them look like clumps of snowflakes on the ground.

The path finally leads onto an area of flat ledges surrounded by slim trees. You have a somewhat limited view through them to the northeast.

Your return from the summit will be by the same route.

38

Camel's Hump

Class: V
Distance (round trip): 7.4 miles
Hiking time: 6 - 6 1/2 hours
Vertical rise: 2,640 feet
USGS 7.5' Huntington; USGS 7.5' Waterbury

At 4,083 feet above sea level, Camel's Hump is Vermont's third highest mountain (tied with Mount Ellen) and rates as one of the finest hikes in the east. Try to climb this peak on a clear day. A mist-and-cloud enshrouded summit is a disappointing reward for the effort expended getting there.

Early French explorers gave the mountain its most appropriate name, the Couching Lion (Le Lion Couchant). From both east and west, its profile does resemble that of a resting lion. Victorians, who quivered at a subsequent name, "Camel's Rump," dubbed the

mountain Camel's Hump.

There are a number of attractive paths to choose from in Camel's Hump trail system, approachable from either North Duxbury or Huntington Center. You can mix and match them to form a hike tailored to your own taste. The combination of trails described here forms a solid day's hiking over the steep, rugged terrain on the mountain's east side.

To reach the start of the Forestry Trail, your route most of the way up the mountain, follow VT 100 south out of Waterbury. Just past the US 2 junction, turn left by the sign for the Duxbury

View of Camel's Hump from the East

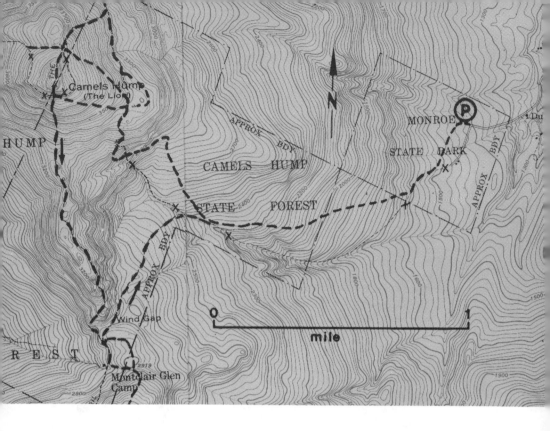

Elementary School. You will pass the red schoolhouse on the right. Continue straight on the gravel road for 5 miles. At that point, a buff-sided, black-roofed barn complex appears on the left. Turn south onto the gravel road just beyond the barns, and follow it 3.5 miles to its end at the Couching Lion Farm parking lot.

Camel's Hump State Park was established in 1969, in hopes of preserving at least one Green Mountain in a natural state. No camping is allowed and no fires are permitted on the trails. Green Mountain Club lodges are available for overnight use for a nominal charge.

At the far end of the parking lot, a pipe bubbles fresh water into a rock-walled well. The water is cold and delicious. If you have fluoridated water in your canteen, change it here.

The Forestry Trail starts beside this watering spot. Marked by pale blue blazes, the trail begins wide and flat. You will soon come to a register box and bulletin board; just beyond, a sign for the Forestry Trail points your way to the left.

The Forestry Trail is well maintained, as are all the trails on Camel's Hump. Long logs are positioned across the path, beside trenched areas, to prevent rain and melting snow runoff from eroding the trail, which is unobstructed by twigs, brush, or litter.

You now make a gradual ascent on the broad packed-dirt trail, although tree roots and boulders sometimes put in an appearance. You will walk over many log bridges; in summer and fall the streams beneath them often dwindle to a trickle or carry no water at all. At 1.3 miles, you reach a set of trail signs. The Forestry Trail goes right, and you are informed that you have 1.8 miles to hike to reach the Long Trail and 2.1 miles to cover to reach Camel's Hump. The Dean Trail, on your left, is where you will come down later in the day.

The trail now becomes much more demanding as it gets rockier and steeper. At 2 miles you will come up to a large and beautiful ledge. You will hike along its left edge until you climb over it. At 2.5 miles the Alpine Trail crosses your path. Yellow blazes clearly mark this route. Stay on the blue-blazed Forestry Trail.

At 3.1 miles the Forestry and Long trails meet in a large grassy clearing. Turn left (south) and follow the Long Trail to the summit. White or white-and-red blazes mark the way as the Long Trail makes a winding, wind-buffeted ascent to the summit of Camel's Hump.

The ten-acre summit of Camel's Hump is one of two arctic-alpine zones in Vermont, the other being Mount Mansfield. The plants and thin soil layer took more than 10,000 years to develop. The most common plant looks like grass, but it is really a rare sedge. Because careless footsteps crush the plants and compact the soil, walk only on exposed rock outcroppings when above treeline. Ranger-Naturalists are on the mountain from May through November to help hikers with any questions they may have about this area and to render assistance if it is needed.

Views extend north and south along the Green Mountains to Canada and Killington Peak, west to Lake Champlain and the Adirondacks, and east to the White Mountains.

After crossing the summit and descending .2 mile, the yellow blazed Alpine Trail leaves the Long Trail to the left. Continue south on the Long Trail. This descent is steep, but you will be rewarded intermittently by views north to the cone of Camel's Hump and east to an eye-stretching vista of mountains and valleys. Underfoot, patches of boggy black mud offer the only relief from nearly continuous rocks and ledges.

As the Long Trail crosses the ridge and descends the east side of the mountain, beaver ponds become visible below. More climbing and sliding down over rock and scrub bring you to the junction of the Dean Trail after 5.1 miles of hiking.

Go left onto the blue-blazed Dean Trail. It is 1 mile from this point to its intersection with the Forestry Trail. The Dean Trail is mostly wet and muddy as it winds through the boggy area abutting the beaver ponds to the left. About .2 mile from the junction you'll come to Hump Brook. The water courses quickly over and around its boulder-filled bed.

At the intersection of the forestry and Dean trails, you are 1.3 miles from the parking area. Turn right onto the blue-blazed Forestry Trail and retrace your route. It is a very pleasant walk back to your car.

39

Mount Hunger

Class: IV
Distance (round trip): 3.8 miles
Hiking time: 4 hours
Vertical rise: 2,259 feet
USGS 7.5' Stowe

Among the highest peaks in the Worcester Range, 3,539-foot Mount Hunger commands superb views. Waterbury Valley and Reservoir nestle serenely to the west. Above and beyond, Green Mountain peaks extend south from Mount Mansfield. In all directions, mountains and valleys stretch before your eyes.

The Waterbury Trail is one of three routes to the summit; the other two begin in Shady Rill and Worcester. Turn off VT 100 at the sign for the Waterbury Center Post Office. Follow this road to its end.

Go left at the stop sign, and then take the first right at the sign for Loomis Hill. Follow this road for 3.4 miles. A parking lot and sign are visible on the right at an abandoned quarry. The blue-blazed trail starts to the left of the quarry, and begins a moderate climb up a rocky path. For the next .5 mile, you will walk through a two-age stand of mixed hardwoods. A few red oak trees are scattered throughout the forest here. At .9 mile, you cross a stream which may (depending on the season) offer you a cool drink.

View from the summit of Mount Elmore to Mount Hunger and the Worcester Range

After approximately 1 mile, look for yellow birches. Both sides of the trail are crowded with these buff-and silver-colored trees. Further along, as if to remind you that they are not to be forgotten, large, smooth-faced white birches dot the way.

The trail now leads up over several long sections of ledge. Water trickles down the path, making it wet and slippery. Red blazes cross the trail, marking the state park boundary line.

The way has become increasingly rock filled and demands careful stepping. The trail swings right, under and around a knoll, and then rises steeply through a maze of white birches. The birch pattern has now been reversed: white dominate, and yellows have been left behind.

Balsam firs begin to appear as the path weaves over a network of roots and crosses a trickling stream at 1.2 miles. Trees are shorter, indicating that you are reaching higher elevations. The path bears left and flattens out for a short distance, providing a respite for wearied legs.

A second, slowly-moving stream crosses the path at the 1.5-mile mark. Pause here for a cooling drink or a soothing footbath in the clear, cold water.

The White Rock Trail leaves the Waterbury Trail on the right .2 mile below the summit.

The dwarfed trees of the higher elevations offer less protection. Temperatures drop and winds blow increasingly stronger. Perpendicular ledge makes the climbing more difficult. Hands and walking sticks must aid your feet here. Hiking becomes a slow, step-at-a-time process.

The summit and surrounding area is barren, except for several dwarfed spruce no more than three feet high. Wind scours the area. (Just .2 mile below the summit another blue-blazed trail leaves the Waterbury Trail on the right.) Stay on the Waterbury Trail when you return.

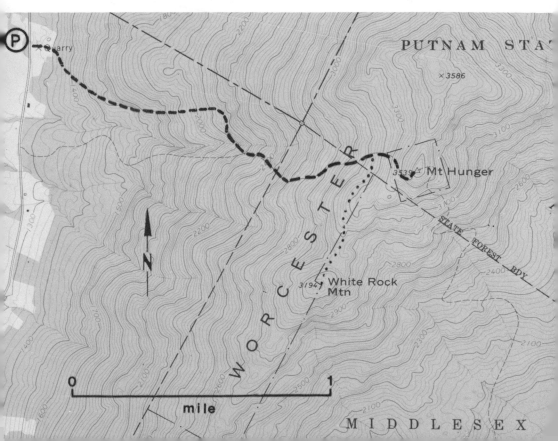

Elmore Mountain

Class: III
Distance (round trip): 3 miles
Hiking time: 2 1/4 hours
Vertical rise: 1,528 feet
USGS 15' Hyde Park

A day or two of varied outdoor recreation awaits you at Elmore State Park. Situated around the shores of Lake Elmore, the park includes a good-sized beach and a hiking trail to the summit of Elmore Mountain. Before or after hiking you'll have opportunities to camp or picnic; go swimming, boating, or fishing; and—if you didn't bring your own food—visit the refreshment stand.

Enter the park from VT 12, 4.3 miles southeast of Morrisville. To reach the hiking trail, go left after paying the small day-use fee at the entrance booth. Go through the picnic area and to the left along an access road which leads uphill to the last picnic shelter. An old fireplace and foundation marks the trail up Elmore Mountain.

The trail begins as a gravel road and winds gradually upward. Varied trees and flowers line the way as the trail becomes slightly steeper. Red blazes on trees to the left appear at the .5-mile mark. Don't mistake them for trail markers; they indicate the state park boundary.

A few steps farther along turn right and walk up the split log steps. Pass between large beech trees with bark scarred by carved initials and names. The trail is wide and comfortable underfoot as it swings to parallel a small brook on the right.

As the way leads upward to the right, occasional log-braced trenches appear. Crossing the path, they divert runoff water before it can build up and damage the trail.

At .8 mile the smooth, flat trail splits. While the path straight ahead looks like the better traveled route, go right, following the steeper, rockier path. Just before you reach a group of large boulders, note that another trail comes in from the left. On your return, remember to stay left at this fork.

The trail winds right and then up to the left. It crosses two areas where logs have been placed atop wet spots. Beyond these logs another path intersects from the left. Just beyond this intersection, logs again provide firm footing across the wet trail. Remember after crossing this last set of logs on the way back that the left trail is the one to take.

The trail is still a pleasant dirt path, relatively free of stones and roots. Steepening as it gains altitude, it goes

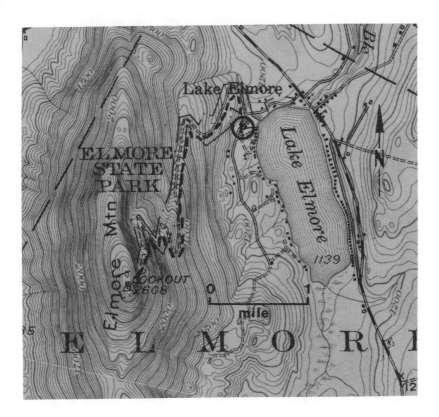

through a wet, muddy area and approaches a high, steep ledge.

Climbing quite steeply, you will top a crest at the 1.2-mile mark and step into a surprisingly picturesque setting: a cleared, grassy knoll overlooking Lake Elmore.

A fine view to the east across Lake Elmore opens from an overlook at the left edge of the clearing. If you are not anxious to climb the very steep and narrow .2-mile trail to the summit, this view provides an acceptable substitute.

The trail follows white painted arrows up the ledge to the summit. Although the climb is very demanding, the reward at the top will make the effort worthwhile.

Climb the lookout tower for a beautiful view. With the exception of the Worcester Range immediately to the south, Elmore Mountain is the highest point in the area. You gaze out over endless miles of rolling hills and manicured farms separated by patches of dark green trees.

The black and white forms of cows dot the open fields and the sun reflects off silos and metal roofs. The impression is one of awesome vastness; the mood, peaceful and relaxed as you look to the horizons.

Return by the same route.

41

Blake Pond

Class: II
Distance (round trip): 5.8 miles
Hiking time: 2 1/2 hours
Vertical rise: 580 feet
USGS 15' Lyndonville

Blake Pond is one of many primitive ponds cradled within Willoughby State Forest's 6,700 acres. The trail to it, like others in the forest, provides a nice opportunity to quietly enjoy nature and, at the same time, limber up your muscles for more strenuous hikes. It also offers an excellent introduction to Willoughby's attractive trail system, where you can easily spend hours.

To reach the Blake Pond Trail, drive to the Willoughby State Forest parking area off US 5. It is located 5.5 miles south of the junction of US 5 and VT 16 in Barton and 7.2 miles north of the junction of US 5 and VT 5A in West Burke. Walk south from the parking lot and turn left onto the dirt road. This trail is not well maintained and may be overgrown in spots. It also may be affected by logging activity.

Follow this road to the sturdy, slatted, wooden bridge crossing the outlet of Bean Pond. If you look southeast across the pond, you'll have a good view of Norris Mountain. Shortly beyond the bridge the dirt road forks. Bear left on the rocky narrow road that makes its way up a small grade. At the top it too forks, and a brown signboard etched with white letters guides you to the right

toward Blake Pond.

Beeches, sugar maples, and white birches parade beside the trail. The way is intermittently dark and light as trees touch branches overhead, blocking much of the sky light. Then they are interrupted by groups of waist-high goldenrod and wood asters. Butterflies and bees dart and swoop among the blossoms.

Much of the way the grade here is steep. The trail turns sharply to the right and continues looping uphill. Watch for the tiny toads that scuttle about your feet (they seem to get underfoot before you notice them).

At .9 mile tall grass and spreading shrubs start to overrun the path as it levels off, giving your muscles a well-earned rest. In another .2 mile, however, you'll climb the steepest grade of this rutted, rocky road. Ferns grow luxuriantly along the trail. Although there are no trail markers, the roadway is so obvious that you won't get lost.

A number of young and mature striped maples fill this area. These slender trees can be readily identified by their large, three-lobed leaves and smooth black-and-white streaked bark.

After 1.7 miles the trail winds to the left

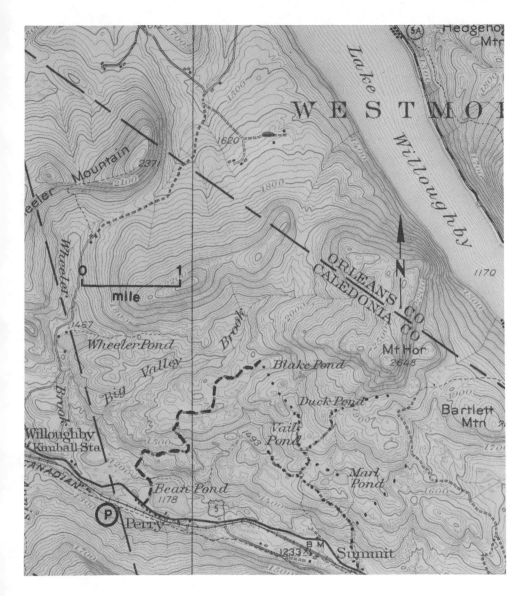

and widens, and the woods become more open. Walking is less arduous than it has been. More brown and white signboards direct you at 2.8 miles. On the right, one points straight ahead to Blake Pond. To the left another aims you to Wheeler Mountain.

The road to Blake Pond, which you follow, forks a short distance beyond the signs, and a sign between the two arms of the fork indicates that you have arrived at the pond. The water is visible through the trees to the right. If you approach quietly, you may surprise a wading blue heron or feeding ducks. If you like to fish, Blake Pond is also a great place to try your newest fishing pole.

Return to your car by the same route.

Mount Pisgah

Class: III
Distance (round trip): 6.9 miles
Hiking time: 4 1/2 hours
Vertical rise: 1,491 feet
USGS 15' Lyndonville

Sheer-faced Mount Pisgah forms the towering southeastern perimeter of Lake Willoughby. Its trails are noted for their prime views of the lake, the northern Green Mountains, and the Burke Mountain-Victory Bog Wilderness. This loop hike takes you up the south side of Pisgah, over the summit, back down the north side, and finally along the base by Lake Willoughby.

The South Trail begins on VT 5A, 5.6 miles south of the junction of VT 5A and VT 16 in Westmore. You'll see the brown and white "South Trail" sign at the eastern side of the highway approximately .5 mile south of Lake Willoughby. Leave your car in the area directly across the road.

The trail leads you down to a couple of well-built log bridges constructed by the Vermont Youth Conservation Corps. Beyond the bridges, the trail is well marked with blue blazes. The wide, relatively smooth path winds its way through brilliant white birches and begins a climb through open woods. Boulders form islands in the trail. Walking is sometimes easy and sometimes rugged, especially over moss-covered rocks. If you believe a favorite uncle's tale about Indian blood causing the rocks to turn green, this area

must have been a major battlefield!

In .2 mile the trail swings ninety degrees to the left at a brown and white sign. The steep grade persists as you pick your way over rocks in the path. The path eventually widens and smooths out, but continues its upward climb.

In .5 mile the trail switches back right, then left, and proceeds up a rocky embankment. Near the top, a 40-foot-long spur on the left leads to the first of the open views from the South Trail. A second area 300 feet farther along offers open western views.

Leaving the second vista, walk upward to the right. Lovely white birch flank the trail, sparkling among the surrounding greens and greys of the forest. At .8 mile, a hand-painted white and black sign guides you to Pulpit Rock, at an elevation of 1,710 feet. Views west are of Mount Hor and Wheeler Mountain; the southern end of Lake Willoughby lies directly below.

The largest fish ever caught in Vermont came from Lake Willoughby's deep waters. On May 8, 1960, Leon E. Hopkins landed a forty-six-inch lake trout that weighed thirty-four pounds and had a twenty-five-inch girth. The fish was so heavy that Leon had to beach it to get it

out of the water. This record specimen can be seen at the Leon E. Hopkins & Son Insurance Agency on Church Street in Lyndonville, Vermont.

The rest of the climb to the summit is unrelentingly steep. It passes over and around boulders and makes a sharp swing left around a massive elm. The white birches give way to beeches and maples, and the path picks its way through stone-strewn areas. At 1.2 miles a medium-sized, blue-blazed boulder bisects the path.

Balsam fir begin to populate the slopes as the grey, broad-leaf forest melds into the green alpine one. Ledge appears and trees become abbreviated in height. Grey mica-flecked sand crunches underfoot as the climb over bare ledge steepens. Natural depressions in the rock and clinging roots provide good footholds. At 1.6 miles you'll be encouraged by a group of signs indicating that the true summit is only 500 feet away. The heavily wooded peak offers no views.

Leave the summit via the North Trail (also blue blazed). About .2 mile from the top you will reach the spur trail to Lookout #1 (West Lookout). Wind your way to the left for awesome views of

Lake Willoughby and surrounding peaks. Mount Hor is the closest to the west. Wheeler Mountain is the rock-faced peak to the northwest. The total view extends sixty miles, from Lake Memphremagog and Jay Peak to Camel's Hump and beyond.

Rejoin the North Trail and continue a short distance to the spur for Lookout #2 (North Lookout). Turn left. White signs with black arrows guide you along this narrow, curving trail.

Retrace your steps to the North Trail and turn left. This cool, shaded path descends gradually. Low bushes threaten to choke portions of it at times. The way becomes steeper and leads over black spongy earth past several massive moss-covered stumps. The path bends sharply to the right and then drops steeply left. At a fork, the Long Pond Trail goes right. Stay on the North Trail to the left. The path descends steeply and rapidly. This is prime ankle-spraining territory, so pick your way carefully.

Finally, at a less extreme angle, the trail courses along a small gully over an old stream bed. At 3.5 miles you must rock-hop across a clear running stream. The trail parallels this stream and turns

View across Lake Willoughby to Mount Pisgah

right as the gurgling quiets in the background. A second stream crosses the path shortly thereafter.

The North Trail continues over gentle hills and gullies. It turns sharply left and begins the steeper descent to VT 5A. Once at the road you have a pleasant 2.7-mile walk along Lake Willoughby to your start.

Devil's Gulch

Class: II
Distance (round trip): 5 miles
Hiking time: 3 hours
Vertical rise: 780 feet
USGS 15' Jay Peak; USGS 15' Hyde Park

This rough gouge in the earth abounds with ferns and moss-covered rocks. It is regarded by the Green Mountain Club as one of the most beautiful, secluded spots of the Long Trail. Its forbidding name adds a primitive lure all its own.

The access road to the portion of the Long Trail leading to Devil's Gulch is VT 118, the Eden-Belvidere Highway. Drive west from Eden 4.8 miles or east from Belvidere Center 6.1 miles. Watch for the green and white Long Trail sign and arrow on the south side of the highway. There is limited parking in a grassy off-road area on the north side of the road. (Hike 44, to Belvidere Mountain, also begins at this point.)

Cross to the road's south side and follow the white blazes of the Long Trail up the embankment and into the woods. The path winds gently through an old pasture which has now grown over with young, mixed hardwood trees. The trail then enters open woods. Its upward course is still gentle, and few roots or stones roughen the way.

A variety of greenery begins to edge the path. One of the most striking specimens is striped maple, with its smooth, greenish bark vividly striped by black and white. In May its clusters of

Deep within Devil's Gulch

yellow flowers appear. The leaves are large, generally with three main lobes.

The trail twists easily up, over, and down gentle knolls. Soon you reach Ritterbrush Lookout, with views of Ritterbrush Pond below, and Bowen Mountain behind. To the left you will see the path dropping down to Devil's Gulch.

This steep downslope may require some careful side-stepping. Generally, you lose elevation on your trek to Devil's Gulch. It's the exact opposite of climbing a mountain: the return trip (via the same route) will be the more trying one.

Soon the path crosses a fast-running stream. This is one of three dependable water sources on the trail. You cross another fast-flowing brook shortly. After winding steeply upward the trail ap-

proaches Ritterbush Camp. This small frame cabin was constructed in 1933 by the Green Mountain Club's Long Trail Patrol and can accommodate eight. (A toilet is provided—up a short trail to the left.) Walk to the back right corner of the cabin and continue hiking.

The way leads steadily upward to a ninety-degree turn where a white sign points left. Here, you may step out onto a small overlook to the right. Below, a stream courses through the middle of a tree-and-shrub-choked gully.

Wind down to the right over a log footbridge into this gully. A miniature waterfall appears to the left. Hold your cupped hands beneath its flow and enjoy a refreshing drink.

Just ahead is a brief but rugged climb

over moss-covered boulders and gnarled roots. The path levels again as stepping stones offer footing across a dank-smelling wet area. Ahead, massive hunks of rock form an A-shaped tunnel. After passing between them, you reach Devil's Gulch.

A jumble of boulders makes hiking a challenge. Above, ledge rises straight and steep on both sides. Ferns feather the surfaces of many of these gargan-tuan boulders. Cave-like depressions lurk among the rocks forming the gulch walls. Stand still and survey these surroundings. The feeling is a primeval one—time seems to have stood still.

The Devil's Gulch is breathtaking—and has a special appeal if you've been climbing a lot of mountains recently. It is such a change. And it even remains attractive in a heavy fog.

Return via the same route.

Belvidere Mountain

Class: III
Distance (round trip): 5.6 miles
Hiking time: 4 hours
Vertical rise: 2,080 feet
USGS 15' Jay Peak

Belvidere Mountain is better known for its asbestos mines than for the expansive views available from its summit. Since 1936, when the Ruberoid Company began systematically mining its slopes, Belvidere has been a leader in producing asbestos. In the mid-1950s this one mountain yielded ninety-six percent of all the asbestos mined in the United States. An active mine at the eastern base of the mountain still supplies asbestos for shingles, cement, theater curtains, firemen's suits, brake linings, pipe coverings, and other products.

This hike begins opposite the one to Devil's Gulch (see Hike 43). The Long Trail crosses VT 118 at the high point of land located 4.8 miles west of Eden and 6.1 miles east of Belvidere Center on the Eden-Belvidere Highway. Look along the south side of the highway for the white and green Long Trail sign. There is limited parking on the north side of the road.

The Long Trail leads into the woods, parallels Frying Pan Brook, and then continues over old VT 118, crossing the fast-flowing brook in the process. As you head into the woods you pass over several wet, boggy areas. Long logs aid

the footing through this thickly muddied section. The path swings upward to the right around a yellow birch and continues to a large maple, which splits the trail. A former logging road leads right and the Long Trail goes left. Keep on the white-blazed Long Trail.

The way steepens moderately, as the gully through which Frying Pan Brook runs appears below to the left. The trail keeps company with the brook for quite a distance, alternately paralleling and swinging away from it.

After .2 mile an old logging road crosses the trail diagonally and dips down to the brook. The brook's waters slither and slide over long stretches of flat rock.

The path intersects another logging road and continues along it to the left. The track suddenly becomes wider and flat. A small trickle of water muddies the trail just before it takes a sharp swing to the right. It leads into a small, low, wet area and seems to stop. Although the trail is not well marked, it goes right here and climbs over root-formed steps.

As the grade flattens out, the trail becomes bumpy with rocks while it parallels the brook on the left. It crisscrosses and rises steeply alongside this miniature wilderness river. The water cascades through slender gouges, over rocks, and into shallow pools before gushing downward again.

More wet patches appear. The path crests a moderate slope and passes over two grassy roads in quick succession. Trail sides overflow with fern, hobblebush, and wood sorrel.

The way becomes very steep as it leads over roots and rocks. Trees thin out drastically at the top of the incline. A startlingly large patch of sky suddenly appears above. You are now approximately halfway to the top of Belvidere Mountain.

Leveling out a bit, the trail crosses an overgrown logging road. Trees become shorter as the way winds upward. It dips down into a small, very wet gully and

finds firmer footing on old logs. You cross still another old road as the trail passes through an open area and weaves left.

Narrowing to a mere footpath, the trail swings steeply right and passes over a long slab of ledge. It tunnels through thick stands of evergreens and is bathed in their fragrance and then picks its way slowly over and around slippery, moss-covered rocks and roots.

Just before a four-way intersection at Belvidere Saddle, between the two peaks of Belvidere Mountain, watch closely for a yellow blaze on the left side of the trail. The unmarked Forester's Trail, your route to the top, is just beyond it on the right, marked with a blue arrow painted on a rock. It brings you in .2 mile to the main summit. The way is very straight and

View of Belvidere Mountain showing the asbestos mine

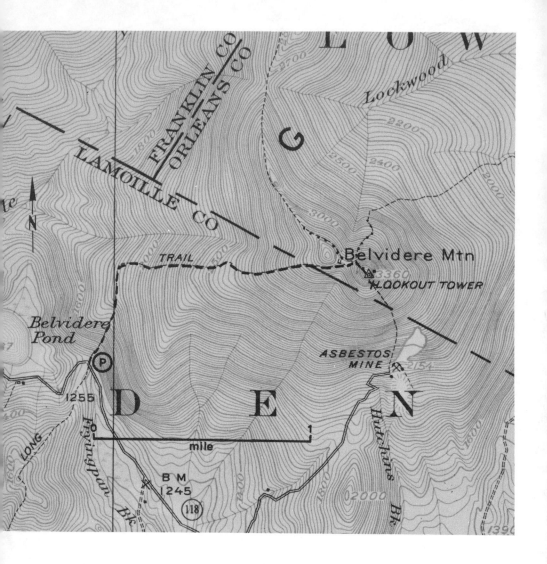

moderately steep.

A lookout tower, recently renovated by the Green Mountain Club, greets you at the summit. Climb the tower and enjoy the unfolding views.

To the east are the peaks around Lake Willoughby: Bald Mountain, Mount Pisgah, and Mount Hor, with the White Mountains of New Hampshire extending to the horizon. Swinging south, the Green Mountains are visible, Mount Mansfield and Camel's Hump, particularly so. The Cold Hollow Mountains sit to the west, while Jay Peak and Big Jay rise prominently in the north. To the right of these twin peaks are Owl's Head and other Canadian peaks in the vicinity of Lake Memphremagog.

Return to your car by the same route.

Jay Peak

Class: IV
Distance (round trip): 3.4 miles
Hiking time: 3 hours
Vertical rise: 1,661 feet
USGS 15' Jay Peak

If you are striving to become a south-to-north end-to-ender on the Long Trail, Jay Peak's summit leaves you only ten miles short of your goal. A primitive wilderness until snow falls, Jay then transforms itself into a bustling center of winter activity as one of the most popular ski areas in northern Vermont. Avid skiers think nothing of traveling hundreds of miles to ride its aerial tramway and make as many runs as time and money allow.

The Long Trail (your route to Jay's summit) crosses the Jay-Montgomery Center Road (VT 242) at the top of a long, steep grade between the two towns. The hike to Jay Peak begins on the north side of the highway, 5.1 miles west of Jay village and 6.7 miles east of Montgomery Center. The Jay Peak Ski area road is 1.3 miles east of this spot.

The Long Trail to Jay Peak, marked by white blazes, begins across the road from the parking area. The Atlas Valley Shelter sits on a knoll just above road level. The Atlas Plywood Division, over whose land the trail passes here, provided this small plywood lean-to. Green Mountain Club members erected it in 1967. It is designed for day use by picnickers and hikers—but it can accommodate three or four people overnight.

The trail begins as a narrow path leading upward through stands of young white birches. After a few minutes' walk, you approach a brown and white sign. The Long Trail continues straight ahead while a side trail leads left to Jay Camp, .2 mile distant.

The way leads upward over an old stream bed. Rock faces are crinkled with moss and tiny pools of water dampen the trail. Beautiful yellow birches suddenly catch your eye as they parade down the hillside and across the path. They glimmer silvery yellow from deep within the woods.

As another side trail from Jay Camp enters on the left, yellow birches begin to mix with the white birches to which they eventually give way. Hobblebush lines the path. Deer like to feed on the twigs and buds of this three-to eight-foot-high shrub. Large white clusters of flowers appear in May and June, while pearl-shaped fruit develop in August and change from red to black at maturity. The leaves also change to a deep magenta color in the fall.

The path leads upward to the left, then dips quickly. Ferns, moss, hobblebush, and striped maple combine to

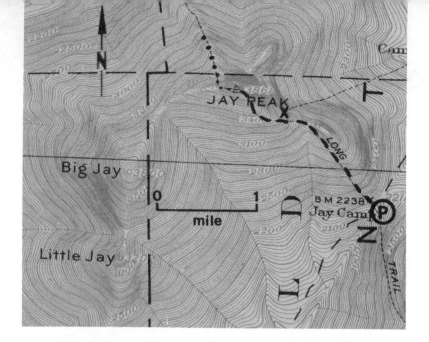

produce heavy green sidegrowth. Slightly higher, common wood sorrel appears near ground level. It has three compound leaves and at a quick glance might be mistaken for clover. Its leaves taste tangy and refreshing.

Edging along the hillside, the slope of the path becomes more gradual. It continues like this for a fair distance, allowing legs and lungs to relax a bit. Then, winding up through spruce and balsam, the way becomes rockier and steeper. Bunches of shining club moss cluster around tree bottoms. They look like small gardens of cactus nestled between the trees.

The Long Trail now approaches and parallels a large ski slope. Damp spots make the going slippery at times. The Christmas-tree smell of balsam fills the air and accompanies you upward.

Just below the summit the way leads out onto a large ski trail cut through the timberland. The 100-foot-wide swath looks like the aftermath of a glacier that flattened everything in its path. Watch closely for white arrows and blazes where the trail crosses the slope and re-enters the woods.

The trail snakes through low scrub growth of spruce and balsam. You pass the small, metal-roofed hut of the ski patrol on the right and begin the final climb to the summit over bumpy ledge and two-foot-high alpine forests.

Cresting the final ledge, you'll find the view is breath-taking, looking out to all directions and taking in rolling hills, towering peaks, flat farmland, winding roads, and long lakes.

Eastward, the view includes Lake Memphremagog; to the west, the Champlain Valley. The Green Mountains can be seen stretching southward as far as Lincoln Peak, while Owl's Head and other Canadian mountains rise to the north.

Your return is via the same trail.

Backpacking Hikes

Stratton Mountain and Pond

Time allowed: 2 days, 1 night
Class: II & III
Distance (round trip): 12.5 miles
Hiking time: 7 hours
Vertical rise: 1,981 feet
USGS 15' Londonderry

Your itinerary for this backpacking trip includes the 3,936-foot south peak of Stratton Mountain, trailside views of beaver ponds, and a night on the shores of Stratton Pond, the largest and one of the most attractive bodies of water on the Long Trail. All in all, it's a great hike.

(Stratton Mountain's north peak, which houses the upper station of the Stratton Mountain Chair Lift, is bypassed on the hike. Should you want to visit this area, follow the .8-mile spur trail leading north from the fire tower on the south peak.)

In 1988 construction will begin on a relocation of the Long Trail from Kelly Stand Road, over the summit of Stratton Mountain, and on to Stratton Pond. The new route will use, in part, the present Stratton Mountain Trail (see the map for the proposed new trail location). The Green Mountain Club and the US Forest Service hope to open the relocation before the end of 1988. Hikers should stay on the alert for changes in the trail markers.

First Day

Arlington-West Wardsboro (Kelley Stand) Road to Stratton Pond.

Class: III
Distance: 5.7 miles
Hiking time: 3 1/2 hours
Vertical rise: 1,616 feet

The Stratton Mountain Trail starts on the Arlington-West Wardsboro Road. Driving east from Arlington to the trail is not recommended, due to rough road conditions. Drive west from VT 100 in West Wardsboro. Signs to Stratton and Arlington mark the turn. After 5.2 miles you'll see the blue blazes for the Stratton Mountain Trail on the right. Just before the trail, there is a small pull-over parking area on your left.

This rather rocky trail soon leads past Webster Shelter at .1 mile. The structure was named for Daniel Webster, who delivered a campaign speech nearby in 1840. At that time, Stratton Mountain rose above one of the most prosperous lumbering and agricultural districts of the state. The Stratton Turnpike added to the area's distinctiveness; it was the road taken by Boston's "best citizens" enroute to summer vacations at

Saratoga Springs.

This prestigious area was selected as the site for a large Whig campaign rally for Harrison and Tyler. A fifty-by-one-hundred-foot log cabin was constructed just off the highway to house the gathering. With Daniel Webster as the orator, the gathering drew a crowd of 15,000 persons (the exact count has been questioned, however, because of the tremendous amounts of hard cider that flowed throughout the proceedings).

Trickling water wets the path as it winds upward at a moderate grade through many evergreens, and at approximately .5 mile the trail crosses a logging road. Beyond this point the path follows a long, direct rise up the side of a hill. The way slides between giant rocks as it leads upward.

Continuing through hardwoods, this well-marked and cleared trail passes just beneath the ridge line on the west side of the slope; then it cuts across the ridge to the east side and bends left. At 1.7 miles, it follows an arrow and makes a sharp swing up to the right.

After a short, steep section, the way resumes its moderate pitch. Grasses and wood asters flourish in open areas. The path crosses a dry brook at 2 miles and turns right just beyond it.

Rougher and steeper, the trail carves its way up through more evergreens. At 2.2 miles a grassy trail forks to the left. Continue straight on the Stratton Mountain Trail.

You emerge onto an old trail at 2.3 miles. Directly ahead a comfortable log bench (the work of some thoughtful person) is situated at just the right spot and welcomes your use. A spring is located here.

You reach the summit of Stratton Mountain after a climb of 2.7 miles. Two small buildings and a fire tower occupy this area. A caretaker may be in residence and would be happy to answer questions, and to name the various peaks you see in the distance. (Please note that camping is not permitted on the summit or elsewhere along this trail, except at the designated shelters.)

Fantastic views await you from the top of the tower. The panorama is unusual, because you are able to see some of the more famous peaks from angles that isolate them against the horizons. Equinox Mountain, highest of the Taconic Range, is on the west. Northeast is Mount Ascutney. New Hampshire's Mount Monadnock dominates the southeastern skyline. South is Somerset Reservoir and Mount Snow. Glastenbury Mountain rises in the southwestern corner.

Beyond and to the left of the tower, the blue-blazed Stratton Mountain Trail descends from the summit. Water seeps onto the path, making the way black and mirey. The grade shortly becomes more gradual as the trail winds down through open woods. After crossing a fast-flowing brook at 3.8 miles, the descent becomes even more gentle and the trail soon crosses a logging road.

Another .5 mile of hiking takes you across a slow-running brook to a beaver pond. Crossing another stream, you can watch its waters flow into yet another pond on the right. As the trail angles left, take time to look for the beaver lodge at the back of this pond.

After winding along above this pond, the way dips down to meet an old road. Swing left and follow the road as it passes through the tall grass of open fields and over two streams. This large clearing was the site of a turn-of-the-century sawmill known as the Dufresne Job. A railroad also passed through this area transporting cut timber to market. With the passage of time this open setting will become a forest landscape. At the 5.2 mile point, branch left at the fork and leave the road. Almost immediately

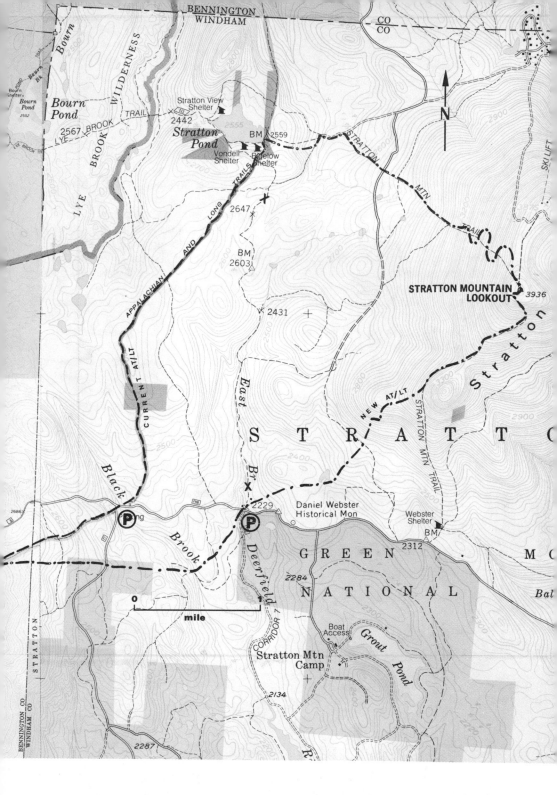

BENNINGTON
WINDHAM

CO
CO

N

Bourn
Bk

Bourn
Shelter

Bourn
Pond
2552

Bourn
Pond

2567

LYE BROOK WILDERNESS

LYE BROOK TR.

LYE BROOK TRAIL

Stratton View
Shelter

2442

Stratton
Pond
2555

BM 2559

Vondell
Shelter

Bigelow
Shelter

STRATTON

MTN

TRAIL

SKI LIFT

APPALACHIAN AND LONG TRAILS

2647

BM
2603

2431

CURRENT AT/LT

STRATTON MOUNTAIN
LOOKOUT

3936

NEW AT/LT

STRATTON MTN TRAIL

Stratton

S T R A T T O

East

Br

Black

Deerfield

Brook

P Parking

196

2686

P

2229

Daniel Webster
Historical Mon

2312

Webster
Shelter

BM

G R E E N

M O

N A T I O N A L

2284

Bal

0

mile

Boat
Access

Grout
Pond

Stratton Mtn
Camp

STRATTON

CORRIDOR 7

2134

2287

BENNINGTON CO
WINDHAM CO

R

you make an angled swing to the right, and the path travels near another beaver pond.

At 5.7 miles you reach Stratton Pond and the Long Trail. Go left on the Long Trail and in 200 feet you reach a clearing where a map of the pond is located and a caretaker is stationed.

Stratton Pond, the largest body of water on the Long Trail, is also the most heavily used location on the trail. From Memorial Day to Columbus Day, more than 2,000 hikers will spend a night at the pond. Such concentrated use can have a serious impact on any environment, particularly the fragile shoreline of a body of water. For this reason, camping is restricted to the three shelters, the North Shore Tenting Area, and the several tent platforms. Fires are also restricted. Please consult the site map or with the caretaker before setting up camp. A small overnight use fee is charged.

Second Day

Stratton View Shelter to Arlington-West Wardsboro (Kelley Stand) Road

Class: II
Distance: 6.8 miles
Hiking time: 3 1/2 hours
Vertical rise: 365 feet

To make your stay at Stratton Pond worthwhile, get up early today. Allow plenty of time for enjoying this scenic spot. You might see early morning animal activity close to the pond's edges. If the weather cooperates, you'll greet the sun as it rises over the mountain and paints the pond red.

When you are ready to depart, circle the pond back to the south, and go to the caretaker's station. From this clearing follow the sign for the Long Trail South. Leaving the pond behind, you climb gradually up over a mixture of rocks and roots.

A sign announcing the distance to the Arlington-West Wardsboro (Kelley Stand) Road stops the trail at .3 mile. The way swings sharply right here and begins a bumpy journey. It dips in spots, but remains fairly level.

View to Stratton Mountain from Bromley Mountain

After a gradual climb the trail levels off again. The thin woods are filled with ferns and shining club moss. Needles cover the trail as you begin to wander through spruces and balsam firs.

There is little change in elevation as the trail log-hops over boggy areas and twists between evergreens. Frequent short dips and rises hinder you from maintaining a steady stride. Don't just pass by the damp boggy areas. These are prime spots for finding animal tracks. Deer, bear, raccoon, bobcat, porcupine — any of these animals might have passed this way recently. Many older, dead trees have visible holes in their trunks. Made either by woodpeckers or branches breaking off, they provide homes for tree swallows, chickadees, nuthatches, wrens, bluebirds, squirrels, raccoons, and martens.

Topping a short slope, the path becomes alternately smooth and rocky. It dips down a short steep bank and spans a large, boggy area atop logs. At 1.6 miles the trail crosses an old grassy road and bears left. After a gradual climb it becomes flatter, smoother, and muddier.

Beginning a long series of bends and straightaways, the trail passes through unchanging woods. This area provides opportunities to do several things while walking along. Try brushing up on tree identification. Many of the hardwoods common to New England fill these woods.

The trail proceeds gradually downward over squishy terrain. Leveling out, the way swings sharply right and drops down to the Arlington-West Wardsboro Highway at 3.9 miles.

Turn left onto the dirt road (it changes to tar farther on). From here you have a 2.9-mile walk back to your car. Unlike the quick dips and rises of the trail, the smoothness of the road will let you stretch your leg muscles. You'll be able to set a good pace from here on.

Middlebury Gap to Brandon Gap

Time allowed: 2 days, 1 night
Class: III & IV
Distance (one way): 9.8 miles
Hiking time: 7 1/2 hours
Vertical rise: 2,535 feet
USGS 7.5' Mount Carmel; USGS 7.5' Bread Loaf

You'll hike up and down five different peaks with continuing panoramas highlighting the way during this two-day trip. There will be plenty of time for stops at the many lookoffs along the trail.

In 1915 Colonel Joseph Battell, an early spokesman for conservation of Vermont's forests, bequeathed to Middlebury College most of the land over which this hike passes. During the late 1800s when his friends were paying thousands of dollars for paintings, Battell was buying thousands of acres of land for $.10 to $.50 cents an acre. As the rates rose, he bought hundreds more at $1.25 per acre.

Responsibility for maintaining this section of the Long Trail (your route for the hike) rests with the U.S. Forest Service, and the Bread Loaf Section of the GMC. The trail is extremely well marked, easy to follow, and well cleared of debris.

First Day

Middlebury Gap to Sucker Brook Shelter
Class: III
Distance: 4.4 miles
Hiking time: 3 1/2 hours
Vertical rise: 1,420 feet

To reach Middlebury Gap, drive 6.4 miles west from Hancock or 5.6 miles east from Ripton on the Robert Frost Memorial Drive (VT 125). The brown and yellow "Long Trail—Green Mountain National Forest" sign on the north side of the road is the landmark to watch for. Across the highway is a large parking area. (You'll finish this hike about 8 miles due south at VT 73; remember to arrange for transportation back to your car.)

From the south side of VT 125, climb the white-blazed Long Trail into the woods. The grade quickly eases as the thin tree cover stretches outward. A ski slope appears through scattered trees to the left, and the path parallels another slope on the right. Continuing moderately upward, the trail crosses intersecting ski slopes and enters the woods beyond. White markers clearly show the way.

The grade becomes more gradual and the walking easier. Suddenly the trail drops and makes a steep descent to Lake Pleiad Shelter. The log steps here were placed to reduce erosion of the trail. You have come .3 mile from Middlebury Gap.

Cross an open ski slope and enter the woods again. The trail flattens out as it passes through thick stands of birches and striped maples and a gathering of spruces.

Long logs carry you across a brook as you approach a trail intersection. The blue-blazed spur to Lake Pleiad exits straight ahead. Turn left uphill, following the white-blazed Long Trail. As the pitch increases the path becomes rougher. Leveling out, the trail intersects an old logging road. The trail skirts a muddy section using occasional log walkways. Watch carefully for the white markers. Cross diagonally to the right and back into the woods. Then follow the arrow to the left.

Rising steeply, the path crosses two more ski trails. From the sloping ledge on the second trail it runs sharply right and zigzags up a steep, roughly cleared slope. At its crest, follow the beaten path up to the left.

The way continues upward to the Robert Frost Lookout, at the crest of the Middlebury Snow Bowl Trail System. The cleared trail offers spectacular views to the east. Mountains near and far seem to roll upon each other like gentle waves.

After a short, moderate climb the path flattens out. It winds cozily through stands of trail-hugging evergreens. With the flatness comes wetness. Boggy areas must be gingerly negotiated.

After dropping over smooth ledge, the dirt path begins a long, moderate ascent over occasional ledge and roots. The aroma of spruce and balsam enlivens your senses.

A slight descent is followed by more level, boggy areas. Beginning another climb, the path rises steeply over ledge and clinging roots. At the top of a sharp pitch, a short trail leads to the right. Follow this spur to a cleared spot offering views of the Middlebury Valley, and of the Adirondacks in the distance. Neighboring peaks sit atop one another as they stretch into the distance. Another .1 mile brings you to the top of Worth Mountain, elevation 3,234 feet. The heavily wooded summit has a narrow slot cut in the firs to allow a brief glimpse of Monastery Mtn.

During the long, steep descent from Worth Mountain, you have occasional views of the Green Mountains stretching southward. Killington Peak is particularly prominent. This entire section of the Long

Sucker Brook Shelter

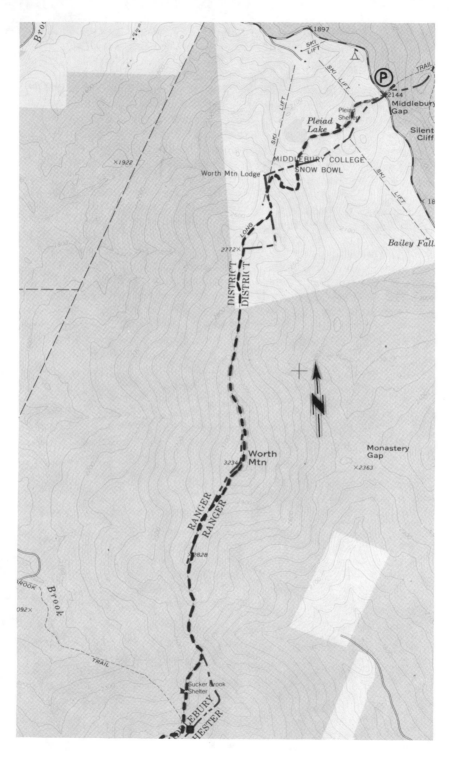

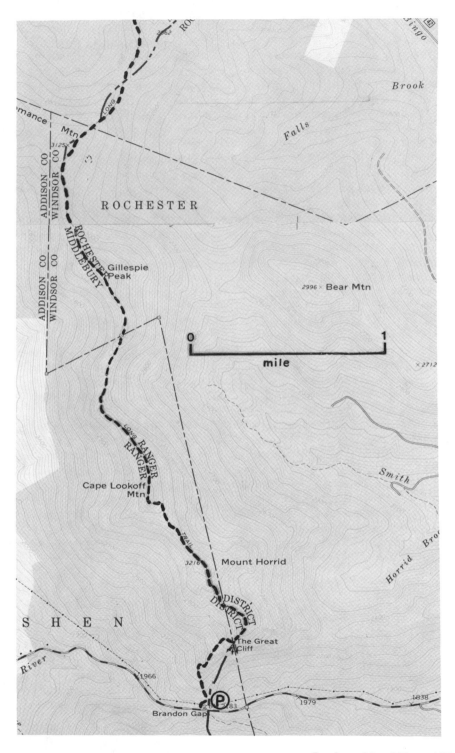

Trail is a haven for partridge. If you are lucky, you might surprise this wise game bird atop a stump or rock while it performs its strutting, spring courtship ritual. More probably, some of them will see you first and rocket upward through thick tree branches. You will often hear the powerful beating of their wings, but never see them at all.

The path levels out after its descent from Worth Mountain. It follows a series of dips and rises and begins a long, gradual descent through the woods. Dropping over a short ledge, the way swings left through a stand of yellow birches. Then hardwood forests flank the path as it rises moderately. Glacial boulders become prominent, and spruces edge the trail as the hillside slopes steeply away.

At 4.3 miles the trail crosses a brook that drains a clear-cut area barely visible through the trees above the trail. This area is rapidly filling in with a dense growth of young trees, which need the open sunlight to get established. The Sucker Brook Shelter is just beyond at 4.4 miles. Its green floor can easily sleep six to eight hikers. Water is available just to the south where Sucker Brook passes under the Long Trail.

The basic rules for use of the shelter include: Put nothing but a clean water bottle in the stream; wash away from the stream; if you have a fire, keep it small and put it out before you leave; and carry out all trash.

Second Day

Sucker Brook Shelter to Brandon Gap.

Class: IV
Distance: 5.4 miles
Hiking time: 4 hours
Vertical rise: 1,115 feet

Before you leave Sucker Brook Shelter, remember to fill your water containers at the brook. Ahead of you today is some steady trekking to four summits and, finally, a rugged descent from the Great Cliff of Mount Horrid.

A short way south of Sucker Brook Shelter, the Long Trail intersects the Sucker Brook Trail. This blue-blazed trail leads west down the valley to a Forest Service road and, eventually, to the Ripton-Goshen Town Road. Stay on the Long Trail.

Making its way to Romance Mountain, the path leads through Romance Gap. Twisting and turning, it climbs steeply over rocks and roots. After cresting this long slope, the path levels out. Shining club moss gleams against the brownish-red carpet of evergreen spills.

A delicious aroma engulfs you as the trail passes through darkened groves of conifers. After more climbing between moss-covered rocks and logs, you emerge onto the eastern summit of Romance Mountain (1.4 miles from Sucker Brook Shelter). There is no view from the tree-covered top of this 3,125-foot peak.

Swing left; the trail drops down off the summit. Very shortly, you come to a fork where a 50-foot spur leads to a western overlook. As you continue south on the Long Trail a view to the east also appears.

Walkalongs aid you through this jumbled area of twisting trail, logs, and roots. This section of the trail follows the ridge line. However, views to the east and west are screened by stands of trees. Occasional spurs lead left and right off the path to overlooks.

After 2.2 miles the narrow trail leads across ledges and upward to the 3,307-foot summit of White Rocks Mountain. From this vantage point you can look to the north and see Romance Mountain. As you begin the descent, green waves of mountains roll south and westward.

The way down is again steep and over rough sections for a bit. The grade then becomes fairly level and proceeds through fir forests. The path moves gradually upward over patches of ledge to another small clearing, the 3,298-foot summit of Cape Lookoff Mountain. A short spur leads west from this heavily treed summit to an overview.

Leaving Cape Lookoff, you wind your way down over more ledges. Continue more gradually downward through stands of birches surrounded by leafy ferns. Then, going up over roots and rocks, you begin a sustained ascent to 3,150-foot Mount Horrid. From here you can look back to Cape Lookoff Mountain and enjoy your recent accomplishment.

The descent from the summit of Mount Horrid to the Great Cliff is a rough one over steep areas of jumbled rock. Walkalongs provide welcome support across particularly boggy areas. There is flatter walking through an area of gnarled birches just before your arrival at the Mount Horrid Lookoff sign (4.8 miles from the start of the day's hiking). Caution rules here. The cliff face drops sharply off and falls 600 feet to the gap below. The highway looks like a slender ribbon as it winds through Brandon Gap. Above it, the Green Mountain chain stretches southward.

Returning from the cliff, go left and follow the white blazes down to Brandon Gap. This .6-mile descent is extremely precipitous in places, dropping very steeply over ledge and roots before leveling out. The sides along the entire descent are forested with sparkling paper birches.

The trail becomes more gradual. After a final easy descent, you emerge from the woods and walk through shrubbery and grass to VT 73. To the east, Rochester and VT 100 are 9.7 miles away; to the west, Brandon and US 7 are 8.2 miles distant.

The Coolidge Range

Time allowed: 3 days, 2 nights
Class: III & IV
Distance (one way): 16.2 miles
Hiking time: 12 hours
Vertical rise: 4,693 feet
USGS 7.5' Killington, USGS 7.5'
* Pico Peak; USGS 7.5' Rutland*

Please note: Due to the National Park Service Appalachian Trail protection program, much of this trail will be rerouted in the future. Please write or call the Green Mountain Club for updates. If writing, send a self-addressed, stamped envelope.

This backpacking trip principally on the Long Trail takes you through the northern mountains of the Coolidge Range. Two of Vermont's most popular peaks are the main attractions here. Pico Peak (elevation 3,957 feet) raises its cone-shaped dome high above Sherburne Pass. South of Pico, Killington Peak (elevation 4,241 feet), the second highest mountain in Vermont, has a more pointed profile.

Most of the steep climbing will be done during the first day and a half. During the second half of this trip, continuous downhill walking puts more strain on the knees than the thighs. You'll have plenty of time for scenery gazing without having to be concerned about hiking time.

First Day

Sherburne Pass to Cooper Lodge
Class: IV
Distance: 5.4 miles
Hiking time 4 1/2 hours
Vertical rise: 3,287 feet

The Long Trail crossing at Sherburne Pass marks the beginning of your hike. Follow US 4 east from Rutland or west from Sherburne Center, to the height-of-land. Overnight parking at the lot on the south side of Sherburne Pass is only by permission from the Inn at Long Trail, located directly across the street. (This trip ends at VT 103 in East Clarendon. You'll have to make plans to return to your car from that point.)

Follow the white blazes south. Don't be fooled by the northward loop. The trail quickly begins a gradual, southerly climb between glacial boulders. After about 500 feet you reach a trail sign. It is 2.3 miles to Pico Camp from here, and 2.7 miles to the Pico summit. The grade be-

On the Long Trail

comes moderately steep as you swing sharply left. Stones fill the path, making the footing less certain.

The trail passes a variety of topographical features as it continues its steady climb. The path gouges into the earth before climbing over roots and ledge. Many spindly young trees fill the woodlands. You pass two huge glacial boulders, both supporting colonies of moss and several trees, on the left. After a looping S-turn, the trail widens and crosses damp, muddy areas.

Partridge thrive all through this section. It's exciting to hear their whirring wings and see the blurred shadows disappearing beyond thick branches. But seeing the small, tufted head and wide, fan-shaped tail close-up is really breathtaking.

The climb from Sherburne Pass has led diagonally upward. At .6 mile the trail crests a low ridge, swings up to the left, and becomes more moderate. As it passes along the east side of the ridge, the pitch lessens still more.

Ferns dominate the forest floor, as you pass through yellow and white birches. The trail crosses to the west side of the ridgeline. Through scattered openings in the now-intermingling white birches and evergreens, you catch glimpses of Pico Peak ahead.

Sink Brook is on the right side at 1.1 miles. Swing left over ledge to the east side of the ridge again. Cut logs help you over a brook at 1.2 miles. Swinging right, the trail begins a long, steady climb. Evergreens predominate, as you walk through and beneath their spreading limbs.

At 1.8 miles you emerge onto Pico's Summit Glade Ski Trail. Proceed upward along its left edge for about 500 feet, then re-enter the woods to the left. A pleasant walk at a fairly constant elevation over the next .4 mile brings you to Pico Camp. Built by the Green Mountain Club's legendary Long Trail Patrol in 1959, this frame cabin has bunks for twelve people. From the clearing here you look south to Killington Peak and southeast to Mount Ascutney.

Behind Pico Camp, the blue-blazed

Pico Loop Trail leads .4 mile to the summit of Pico Peak. This narrow, winding, and sometimes steep trail brings you through mature spruce and fir to a ski area work road. Head 50 feet up the road, then bear right at the blue blaze. Soon you will emerge on a ski slope and continue to ascend, passing a ski patrol cabin on your left, and beneath the main Pico Chairlift.

Ahead to the right is a wide, bare path leading to the summit. Microwave towers welcome you at the top. Primary views extend to the north and south. Killington Peak fills the area to the southwest. On leaving the summit, retrace your previous route under the chairlift and back to Pico Camp. This is the halfway point of today's hike and a good spot to rest awhile. A spring is located 100 feet to the north on the Long Trail.

Below, to the right of Pico Camp, the Long Trail South begins a very long, gradual descent. For approximately 1 mile you hike along the west side of the ridge and enjoy the gradual ups and downs in the trail. One heavily rooted section offers the only change from the surprisingly comfortable going.

Soon, a steeper descent leads to a raised walkalong. Boggy areas lie ahead. Rocks and logs help you through them.

Killington looms ahead. At 3.9 miles a sign informs you that you are now halfway between Pico Camp and Cooper Lodge. You've only 1.5 miles left today.

The Long Trail has been relocated to the west side of Snowden Peak. Signs mark both ends of the change. No longer does the trail pass by the Snowden lifts. Enjoy the uninterrupted wilderness walking.

Your first noticeable climb since leaving Pico Camp begins at the northern end of the route. The grade rises steeply over rivers of rocks and flattens out only occasionally along this revised section.

Approaching the Killington West Glade

Ski Trail, the path swings right. Rocks and crusty roots make the footing wobbly. You cross several small brooks and walkalongs before reaching an iron pipe that drips spring water onto the trail at 5.3 miles.

Cooper Lodge is just ahead. This attractive shelter was constructed in 1939 by the Vermont Forest Service and extensively repaired in 1969 by the Vermont Department of Forests and Parks. The floor and most of the walls are stone. A picnic table, and bunk space for twelve to sixteen people will make you comfortable tonight. Springs are located 100 feet south of the lodge.

Second Day

Cooper Lodge to Governor Clement Shelter

Class: III
Distance: 4.5 miles
Hiking time: 3 1/2 hours
Vertical rise: 610 feet

This day will include an ascent to Killington Peak. (The town that was once its namesake is today known as Sherburne.) A vast 360-degree view from Killington's summit is sure to impress you. Ascutney rises most prominently to the southeast. The White Mountains of New Hampshire are visible in the northeast. To the west are Mendon Peak, the City of Rutland, Lake Champlain, and the Adirondacks of New York State. You look down on the summit of Pico Peak to the north.

From Cooper Lodge take the Long Trail South. Folow its white blazes approximately 100 feet to a small clearing. Here the blue-blazed spur to Killington Peak leads east off the Long Trail. This .2-mile spur to the summit is a steep climb over jagged pieces of rock and ledge. Scrub growth edges the trail. Your first view of the top includes a lookout tower (not open to the public) and a radio installation. A spur to the east takes you to the Killington Gondola Terminal and Restaurant.

When ready to resume your back-packing journey, descend to the Long Trail via the Killington Peak spur and go left (south). The path follows an easy grade along the southwest slope. It is possible to maintain a smooth and spirited stride over this undemanding section of trail. Spruce and balsam spills give the path its "bounciness."

You start an extended gradual descent .8 mile from the start of today's hike. There's a quietness about this evergreen-rimmed path. Kneel to examine the cloverlike clumps of wood sorrel. On an autumn morning their three-part compound leaves may be delicately outlined by frost. Chickadees abound.

Near a clump of wood sorrel there may be a group of "creeping evergreens." Shining club moss is the species that predominates here. Tiny, bright-green, pointed leaves encircle its erect stalks.

A gradual descent over a rocky path leads to a crossing of Killington's Juggernaut Ski Trail, and shortly after, a junction with the blue-blazed Shrewsbury Peak Trail. (This side trail goes 2 miles southeast to the summit of Shrewsbury Peak, and beyond.) Continue on the white-blazed Long Trail, crossing the Juggernaut Ski Trail once again. The path maintains its gentle trend as it crosses the east slope of Little Killington. At 1.8 miles you reach Consultation Point, elevation 3,750 feet.

After leaving Consultation Point, the trail slices along the south slope of Little Killington. It becomes narrower and very rough as it winds around trees and over roots and rocks. To the left, the hillside slopes off steeply. Ever so slowly, you make your way downhill.

After crossing two small streams, the Long Trail swings sharply right at 2.6

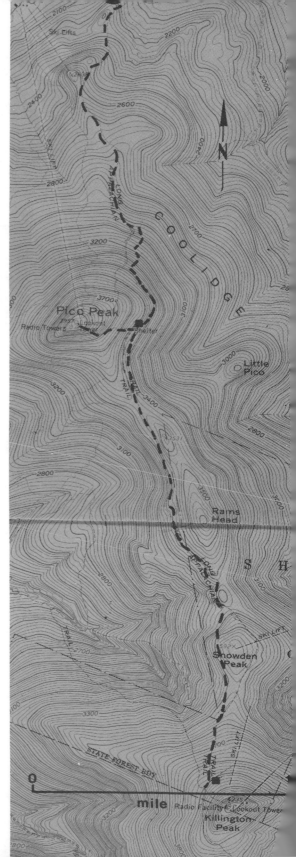

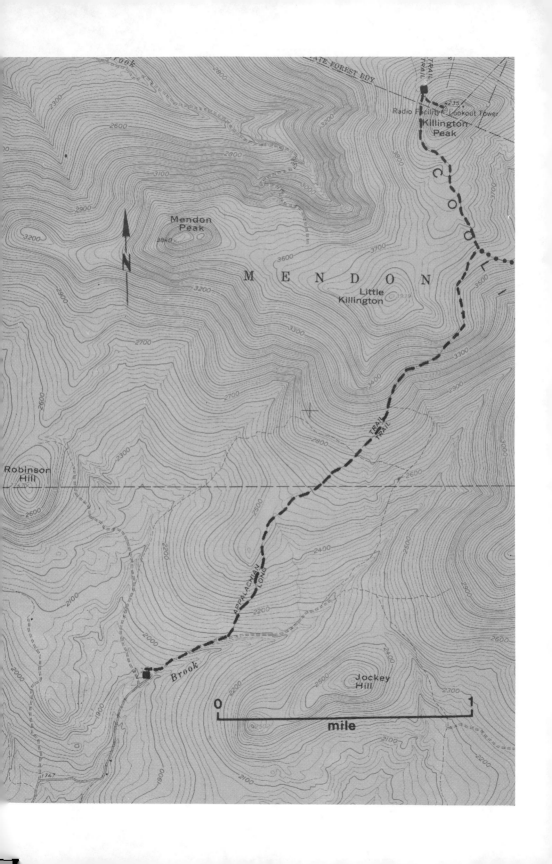

miles. You have an easy, level walk once again. Oak and beech are prominent in the deciduous forest to the sides of the path.

Such open woods as these are the blue jay's favored habitat. This handsome bird has an assortment of voices, ranging from raucous calls to melodious warbles. Blue jays include insects in their summer diet, but they are primarily vegetarians. Interestingly, they perform an important reforestation service. By burying more acorns and beechnuts than they ever can eat, they help plant new trees.

About .5 mile from the last sharp turn, you cross a walkalong and turn sharply left onto an old road. Very quickly, you turn right off this road and continue on a path twisting through open woods.

Soon the trail crosses a road. It proceeds downward through more woods and emerges onto still another old road. It follows this one awhile before branching right onto a rocky, gutted path.

At 4.2 miles this trail descends some sturdy log stairs and joins a logging road. Follow it to the right. A rushing brook parallels the way on the left. Ahead you can see the roof of the Governor Clement Shelter.

The William H. Field family of Mendon erected this shelter in 1929. It bears the name of Percival W. Clement, who governed Vermont from 1919 to 1921. Its deep-set bunks accommodate eight to ten persons. A picnic table and stone fireplace add luxury to the comfortable setting.

Third Day

Clement Shelter to VT 103

Class: III
Distance: 6.6 miles
Hiking time: 4 hours
Vertical rise: 790 feet

Two steep climbs to hilltops interrupt, and add diversity to, today's long, gradual descent. The walking is easy; you will have time to enjoy the surroundings.

From the shelter, the white-blazed Long Trail bears west, passes a dirt road, and crosses Robinson Brook on a footbridge. The sound of running water accompanies you as the trail bears south high above the brook. After .4 mile a small clearing is reached. It is hard to imagine that this was once the site of the Herb Haley farm, described in GMC's 1920 *Guide Book of the Long Trail* as a place where hikers could find bed, board and a telephone.

A driveable country lane is reached at 1.8 miles. Turn left onto this road, crossing a bridge over a stream, then follow the white arrow into the evergreens just after the bridge. The flat trail dips down to the edge of the roaring stream. The steep hillside closes down to the path. Step carefully over the slippery roots along this very narrow part of the trail.

Yellow birches lead into thick evergreens as the path swings away from the water. Upper Road interrupts the tranquility at 1.4 miles—but only until you re-enter the woods on the other side.

The trail continues flat and narrow. It crosses several small brooks and many boggy areas. Few logs or walkalongs aid your travel in these muddy sections.

Look to the sides of the trail for the firmest footing.

Much of the path is sandy as you continue within sound of the stream. The path winds along next to the water again. Such airy openness offers a nice change from the narrow, tree-lined trail. Rising steeply from the water's edge, the way leads over a hogback. It's a little like walking over a natural bridge. Streams rush by far below on both sides, as the straight path passes beneath towering evergreens.

The trail drops down to a dry brook bed and follows it to a junction with a wide stream. Pick your route and rock-hop across. Then switch back to the left and climb steeply up away from the stream.

You pass along a shelf high above the stream, which has now grown much larger, to your right. The Long Trail descends and bears left from the stream at 2.7 miles. A clearing and rutted drive that provides access to a mobile home is reached. Follow the drive, then enter the woods again at the white arrow on the right and continue out onto Cold River (Lower) Road at another mobile home. Go right, cross the bridge, and turn left off the road. Ascend to a clearing, cross a gravel road, and continue your ascent through the woods.

A long, steady climb brings you to the top of the ridge. You're likely to see golden-crowned kinglets anywhere along here. These tiny (three-to-five-inch) birds are a dull, olive-grey color, with golden crowns bordered by black and white. They can be seen feeding on branches of firs, spruces, or other conifers. Like the black-capped chickadee, they will often fly close to look you over.

The way descends from the ridge and passes over more boggy areas, before reaching Hermit Spring at 4.5 miles. During dry seasons, though, water may not be available here.

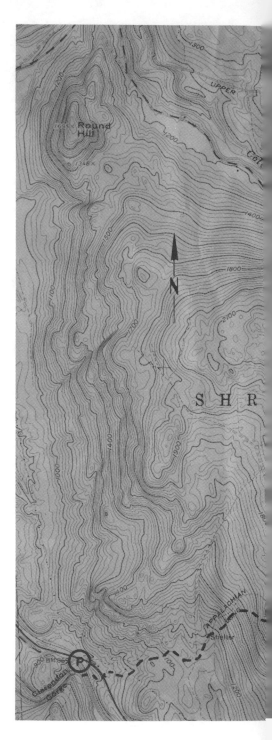

Just after crossing the corner of a rocky pasture, the path winds through some unusual trees. These tamaracks (American larches) are northern conifers that shed their leaves in the fall. Short needles grow in tufts at the ends of abbreviated branches, giving the tree a spidery look. Tiny, scaly cones sit upright. Its tough root fibers were used by eastern Indians to bind birch bark canoe seams. Grouse, hares, red squirrels, porcupines and deer eat the seeds, needles, and inner bark.

The trail passes through the pasture again and crosses Lottery Road at 4.9 miles. It ascends steeply over rocks and smooth ledge to Beacon Hill. The elevation of this grassy knoll is 1,740 feet. Keep to the left of the signed telephone pole and begin the steep, winding descent.

The rocky descent culminates at Clarendon Shelter after 5.8 miles. The trail passes left of the shelter through the cleared area and swings right to a stone wall. Step over it onto the dirt road and go left. This flat road bears right at a fork and leads .8 mile to VT 103. A granite monument marking the historic Crown Point Military Road of 1759, is where your backpacking trip terminates.

The Presidential Range: Lincoln Gap to Middlebury Gap

Time allowed: 3 days, 2 nights
Class: III & IV
Distance (one way): 17.7 miles
Hiking time: 13 hours
Vertical rise: 4,457 feet
USGS 7.5' Lincoln; USGS 7.5' Bread Loaf

Each of the eight mountains included in this north-to-south trip rises over 3,000 feet (the highest is 3,835 feet). From their summits and trails you'll see the New Haven River Basin with its semi-circle of towering peaks, the wide Champlain Valley, and a vast variety of mountains. Among this quiet splendor you'll bed down just above an isolated pond high on a mountainside. To enjoy all this to the fullest, make sure you've limbered up any rusty muscles well in advance.

This backpacking journey takes you over "Presidential Peaks" from the Lincoln-Warren Highway to VT 125. The U.S. Forest Service does an excellent job of maintaining the trails. They are free from windfalls and obstructions.

First Day

Lincoln Gap to Cooley Glen Shelter

Class: III
Distance: 4.7 miles
Hiking time: 3 1/2 hours
Vertical rise: 1,896 feet

The access road for this trip is the Lincoln-Warren Highway. Drive from either Lincoln or Warren to the height-of-

land. Ample off-the-road parking is available here. (You'll have to work out a way back to your car when the hike ends at VT 125.)

On the south side of the highway, climb steeply out of Lincoln Gap to the east side of the ridge. The steeply sloping trailsides are forested with birches, beeches, and maples. At .4 mile you come to Eastwood's Rise, where you get your first view of the day.

Continue south along the ridge, still in the hardwood forest. Occasional clusters of ferns fill the forest to either side. Finally, at 1.1 miles, you come to Sunset Ledge. To the west, you have a panoramic view across Lake Champlain to the Adirondacks in the distance.

Still following the ridgeline, continue south with easy ups and downs, then begin to climb steadily as you ascend Mount Grant. As you climb higher, the birches and other hardwood trees are replaced by spruce and fir.

Picking your way over loose rocks and tangles of roots, you climb the steep east ridge. Intermittent views of near and far mountains appear through the trees. Needles carpet the way as the delicious aroma of spruce and balsam engulfs you.

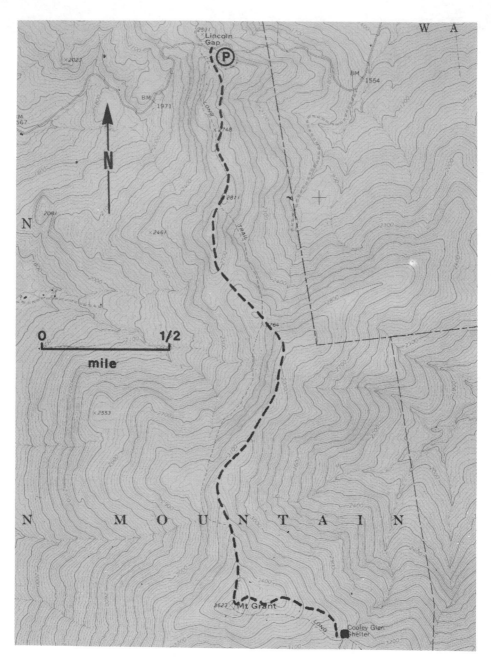

After ascending areas of packed dirt and ledge sandwiched between shorter evergreens, you emerge onto level ledge: the summit of Mount Grant, elevation 3,623 feet. Signs direct you to the right for a close vista, which includes Mounts Cleveland, Roosevelt, and Wilson and Bread Loaf Mountain.

Beyond, to the south and southeast, are Killington Peak and Mount Ascutney.

It is .8 mile from here to Cooley Glen Shelter. You wind your way down from the summit between stands of trail-hugging evergreens. Directly ahead Mount Cleveland comes into full view. Soon the path curves to the southeast and the slope lessens, making for easier walking. The way widens and continues through a great stand of fir and spruce to Cooley Glen Shelter.

This frame lean-to, erected in 1965 by the U.S. Forest Service, has room for six to eight people and will see you through your first night. Branching right from the Long Trail South just beyond the shelter, the Cooley Glen Trail leads 500 feet to a spring.

Second Day

Cooley Glen Shelter to Skyline Lodge

Class: IV
Distance: 7.8 miles
Hiking time: 6 hours
Vertical rise: 1,966 feet

As you can see by checking the distance, today you will have a full day of hiking. Much of it is up and down an assortment of peaks. You'll want to be well rested and get an early start.

Leaving Cooley Glen Shelter, the Long Trail South climbs very steeply to the east. Twisting and turning, the path becomes moderate and even gradual as it passes through stands of balsam and spruce. The footing is rooted at times but rock-free. After a quick .5 mile, you arrive at the heavily wooded summit of Mount Cleveland, elevation 3,482 feet. No views.

Descend gradually along the east ridge. A short climb brings you across to the west side. Descending again, you pass through hundreds of handsome white birches interspersed with evergreens. This long descent offers occasional views of the other peaks you'll be visiting today. Stretching southward before you are Mounts Roosevelt and Wilson and Bread Loaf Mountain.

The contorted black skeletons of aged, dead trees dot the lower stretches of open woods. Their rough, shingled bulks rise imposingly among the younger surrounding trees. Shelves of mushrooms and fungi thrive on their surfaces.

The trail begins a moderate climb. It flattens out again, then rises gradually and begins a long traverse to the east. Becoming steeper, it swings right and returns to the west side of the ridgeline.

Crossing the ridge on a long, flat cut eastward, the path reaches the summit of Little Hans Peak at 2.1 miles. A wood sign gives the elevation as 3,400 feet.

Leading east from this summit, the path passes over occasional roots and a few rocks. Firs and spruces continue to perfume the air and spill needles on the trail.

At 2.4 miles from the beginning of the day's hiking, you cross a trickling brook and then climb easily to another long, wet, log-crossed area leading west. The trail winds back to the east and rises to a rocky overlook before crossing Mount Roosevelt's 3,528-foot summit. Descending in a southerly direction, Mount Wilson and Bread Loaf mountain are visible at close range straight ahead.

The path gradually climbs, then drops. Step carefully over ledge and loose rocks as you go steeply downward. At the bottom of this slope the Clark Brook Trail leads left to Granville.

The trail now begins a long ascent to Mount Wilson. You wonder at times where the peak is as the path descends over rocks and roots. Turning sharply left, the way scrambles moderately up over narrow ledge. Keeping to the east of the ridge, you make your way to the peak.

At the 4.8-mile point, you arrive at

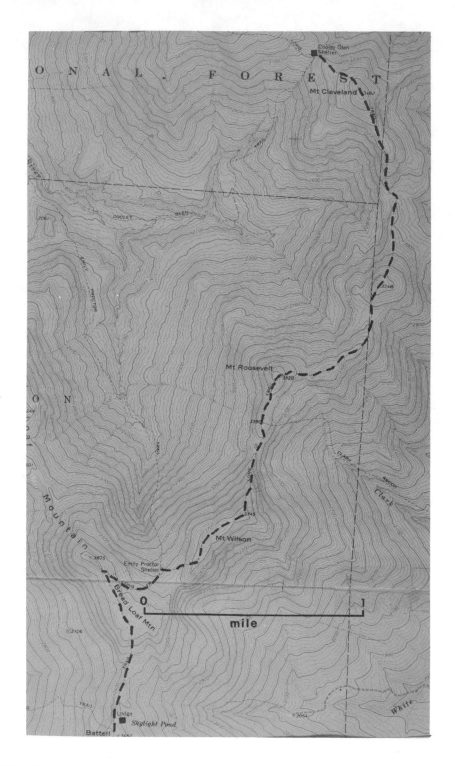

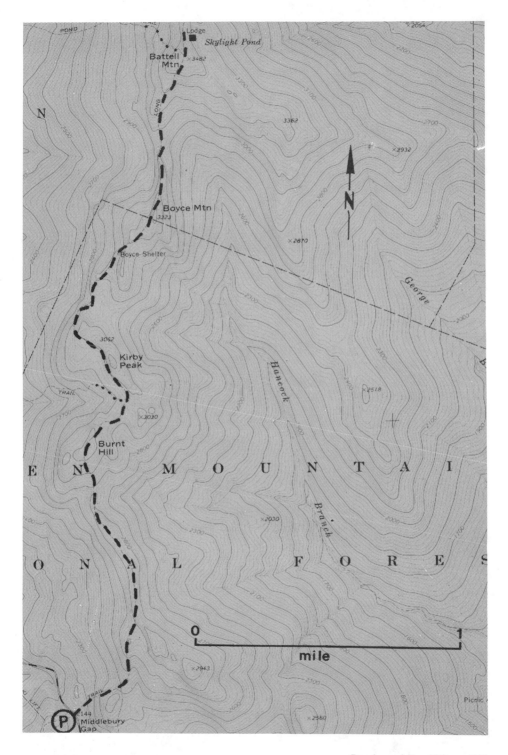

Mount Wilson, elevation 3,745 feet. The Long Trail leads to the right from this wooded summit. Before continuing, follow the short spur straight ahead for far-reaching views to the east and south.

Leaving Mount Wilson, the trail begins a short series of descents and ascents. It then starts a very long steep descent to Emily Proctor Shelter. Stepping down over precipitous sections of rocks and roots, you reach the shelter.

The Long Trail bears sharply left, crosses a brook, and passes upward over wet ground and rocks. At the 6.3-mile mark you enter a clearing containing a number of signs. The Long Trail makes a switchback left. Climb the right spur to the vista on Bread Loaf Mountain. You'll want to spend some time enjoying the expansive view across the Champlain Valley from this 3,835-foot vantage point.

Return to the clearing and proceed south. An interesting sign stops you after a short walk. Although probably not as meaningful to you as to a striving end-to-ender, it informs you that you are now at the midpoint of the Long Trail—equidistant (130.4 miles) from the Massachusetts and Canadian borders.

Step down over a damp path. Long cut trees minimize the chances of sinking into the mud. Ledge marks the start of a very steep section.

Entering a clearing, you come to the Skylight Pond Trail. The trail leads right toward Ripton and left to Skylight Pond. Follow the blue blazes to the lodge and pond. This fine log cabin was built in 1987 to replace the original lodge.

This picturesque spot rewards your long day's hike. The lodge sits on a bluff overlooking Skylight Pond. From its raised porch you look across the tree-enclosed pond to distant peaks. With bunk and loft space for twelve, plus water at a nearby spring, you should be quite comfortable here.

Third Day

Skyline Lodge to Middlebury Gap

Class: III
Distance: 5.3 miles
Hiking time: 3 1/2 hours
Vertical rise: 575 feet

This last day of your backpacking trip offers an interesting assortment of hiking and visits to many overlooks. Climb up

Massive birch over the Long Trail

the steep trail behind Skyline Lodge to the brown-and-yellow sign directing you left to the Long Trail South. Go left and follow the white blazes.

At .2 mile on the Long Trail you pass over Battell Mountain. The elevation is 3,482 feet, but the heavily wooded summit does not provide any views. The gradual ups and downs of the trail frequently lead over boggy areas. Walkalongs aid your passage over these muddy sections.

After 1.2 miles your route passes a trail to the right for the Boyce Lookout. It leads 20 feet to a partial overlook to the west. A bit further, you cross over the wooded summit of 3,323 foot Mount Boyce.

The Long Trail makes a fairly long, gradual descent, reaching Boyce Shelter after about 1 mile from the Boyce summit. It resumes behind the shelter and rises steadily, before leveling out and maintaining a rough route over the rocks, slippery ledge, and roots of the west slope of Kirby Peak.

The Burnt Hill Trail joins the Long Trail after another .7 mile. This path, main-tained by the Bread Loaf section of the GMC, leads 2.1 miles down to a forest service road; 4 miles from Ripton. Continue on the white-blazed Long Trail South.

At the 3.2-mile point in today's hike, after a short ascent, you reach the rounded, ledged area called Burnt Hill. Follow the trail as it leads sharply left off the hill.

The now gradual trail makes a long descent through thin forest. In the process it crosses the ridge from west to east. Occasional climbs over gnarled roots onto ledged areas vary the hiking. After descending a long, moderate slope you come to a sign pointing left to the Silent Cliff Trail. From the cliff there are views to Monastery and Middlebury gaps.

The Long Trail swings sharply right from this intersection and makes a long, steep descent over two sets of log steps, which prevent trail erosion. After leveling out, it rambles briefly through the woods before emerging onto a small embankment above Robert Frost Memorial Drive (VT 125) at Middlebury Gap.

50

Mount Mansfield

Time allowed: 5 days, 4 nights
Class: IV & V
Distance (around loop): 17.2 miles
Hiking time: 16 1/2 hours
Vertical rise: 6,110 feet
USGS 7.5' Mount Mansfield

Much folklore has been woven around the origin of Mount Mansfield, Vermont's highest peak. One tale has it that a chap named Mansfield was pitched off Camel's Hump when the beast stumbled while kneeling to drink. He lies, stone-faced, staring at the sky and giving the mountain its famous profile. Another story claims that it is the profile of Mishawaka, crippled son of an Indian chief, who perished on Mansfield's summit after crawling there to prove his courage and uphold his family's honor. Several stormy days followed his death, during which the mountain changed from one peak to the outline of Mishawaka's face.

There's a story about the naming of the mountain, too. The Abnaki Indians first christened it "Moze-o-de-be-Wado," meaning "Mountain-with-a-head-like-a-moose." Its present name is derived from that of an English Chief Justice, Lord Mansfield, whose name also graced the town (now Stowe) that sits not far from the mountain's base.

The following backpacking trip will take you to most of the mountain's famous points of interest. All the sections of its distinctive profile are included: Adam's Apple, Chin, Lower Lip, Upper Lip, Nose, and Forehead. You will also visit the Lake of the Clouds, Wall Street, the Canyon, the Subway, and Wampahoofus Rock.

Our route is chosen from the system of trails webbing Mount Mansfield. It includes some of the most rugged trails in Vermont, as well as the highest point, the Chin, elevation 4,393 feet. Variety is provided by underpasses, switchbacks, crevices, caves, and ladders.

The mountain's trail system is maintained by the Green Mountain Club, the University of Vermont Outing Club, and by the Vermont Department of Forests, Parks, and Recreation. All the side trails are blazed in blue, while the Long Trail is blazed in white. Above tree line, the Long Trail blazes are white with a red boundary. Trail signs are posted at all junctions.

The Green Mountain Club also maintains the Taft and Butler lodges, where you will spend your nights on the mountain. Caretakers are stationed at these lodges, and a small fee is charged for their use. There are no fires allowed on Mount Mansfield, so be sure to bring a small backpacking stove.

Mount Mansfield also has Ranger-Naturalists in residence from May through November to assist hikers in emergencies, and to help answer questions they might have. The rangers ask that while hiking above the treeline you stick to the blazed trails and walk only on the exposed rocks. Mount Mansfield is one of only two arctic-alpine areas in Vermont. With increased use and accessibility this 250-acre area is being destroyed more quickly than it can regenerate itself. What appears to be grass around you is actually a tight-knit community of arctic-alpine sedge and belongs to the seventeen endangered species growing on the mountain. These plant communities, and the underlying soil, have developed slowly in the 10,000 year period since the retreat of the last glacier. Footsteps can easily destroy this fragile vegetation and leave the soil open to erosion, so *please* walk carefully and only on the paths.

For more information on Mount Mansfield and its many trails, consult the Green Mountain Club's *Guide Book of the Long Trail*. A four color, fold-out map of the mountain comes with the book.

First Day

VT 108 to Taft Lodge, Adams Apple, and Lake of the Clouds

Class: III
Distance: 2.8 miles
Hiking time: 4 hours
Vertical rise: 2,460 feet

The Long Trail, one of the nation's oldest long distance hiking trails, will lead you up Mount Mansfield to your first night's destination. To reach the Long Trail, drive north from Stowe on VT 108 past the Mount Mansfield and Spruce Peak Ski Areas, until you see the white and green sign for the Long Trail on the left. Parking is just beyond in a pull off on the left. From RT 15 in Jeffersonville, follow VT 108 South 1.8 miles beyond Smugglers Notch.

A large bulletin board greets hikers at the trailhead with information about the mountain. One sign notes that adequate rain gear, warm clothing, and a flashlight are of primary importance. Others mention the arctic-alpine plants, rules and regulations, and information of general interest. Almost 10,000 people follow the Long Trail to the summit of Mount Mansfield each year.

The white-blazed Long Trail climbs moderately through a maple and beech forest. Watch for the hairy woodpeckers who make their home here. Older spruce and hemlock add diversity to the hardwoods. The trail approaches a large brook, only to veer to the right and climb. When the brook is reached a second time, a register box attached to a tree marks the 0.5 mile point. The trail again turns upward to the right before it levels off, reaches the brook again, and finally crosses it. Here is a cool spot to rest.

From the brook, the climbing is steady, but not difficult. Birch trees, spruce, and fir begin to fill the forest as you go higher up the mountain. One half mile from Taft Lodge the trail approaches a ski slope, and then turns right and climbs steeply. Suddenly, at 1.7 miles, a large log cabin appears before you.

Taft Lodge is the largest and the oldest shelter on the Long Trail. Built in 1920, it has bunks for 32 people and is the highest use shelter on the trail. Because camping away from the shelters is not allowed on the mountain, you will be sure to have company for the night.

The GMC has a Caretaker stationed at Taft Lodge to work on nearby trails and to help hikers to minimize their impact on the site. If the Caretaker is not present when you arrive, signs inside the shelter will tell you where to get water, and how to use the washpit and the composting outhouse.

At long last you can drop your packs in the shelter! Taft Lodge, at 3,650 feet,

is an ideal starting point for exploration of the mountain's other hiking trails. A loop hike to the summit using the Long Trail and the Profanity Trail takes about 2 hours and can be done easily in an afternoon. The short afternoon hike we suggest here will take you to the Adam's Apple and Lake of the Clouds, two of the most beautiful and least visited spots.

From Taft Lodge, follow the rocky Long Trail upward .3 mile to Eagle Pass. The Long Trail to the Chin goes left. To the right are the Hell Brook Trail, and the Adam's Apple Trail. Go right. For an interesting loop start up the Adam's Apple Trail which is marked by blue blazes and rock cairns. The Adam's Apple, at 4,060 feet, is the third highest point on Mount Mansfield. The Chin looms to the south. Arctic-alpine plants such as bog bilberry, a low, heath-like plant, surround you. In late June and early July, many small flowers are in bloom.

Cross over the Adam's Apple, and descend to the junction of the Hell Brook Trail and Bear Pond Trail. Go straight ahead on the Bear Pond Trail. Soon, a short side trail leads to the left to the Lake of the Clouds, the highest permanent body of water in Vermont.

From here it is .9 mile to Bear Pond, a walk along the ridge which will take you about half an hour. If you choose this extra side trip, you will be rewarded with several striking views of Smuggler's Notch along the way.

Returning to the junction of the Hell Brook Trail, go right and follow it until you reach the junction of the Long Trail at Eagle Pass. The Chin rises strikingly before you. Return to Taft Lodge via the Long Trail.

Second Day

Long Trail to the Chin, Cliff Trail-Canyon Trail Loop

Class: V
Distance: 4.9 miles
Hiking time: 4 1/2 hours
Vertical rise: 1700 feet

If the day is clear, and you rise early, the sunrise is yours. With a good night's rest behind you and a hearty breakfast under your belt, you are ready for today's trails. You will pass over very little level ground!

Since you will be returning to Taft Lodge for the night you will want to take along a day pack and stow your backpack in the corner of a bunk. Be sure to bring plenty of water with you, as well as your lunch, rain gear, a sweater, first aid kit, and a flashlight (there are some caves along the way).

From Taft Lodge walk back up the Long Trail .3 mile to Eagle Pass. Go left and along the Long Trail. You will walk up over boulders and ledge. The path swings left around a sheer rock face, goes up through a narrow crevice, and then intersects the Story Trail (save this scenic trail for tomorrow).

The climbing becomes steeper as you rise above the tree line and look almost straight up toward your goal: The Chin. Cresting the north end of the ridge you realize how high you are! Behind you to the north is the Adam's Apple and the Lake of the Clouds. A short distance further and you will reach the summit, identified by a USGS marker. The Chin is the highest point in the state—the top of Vermont. Take time to enjoy both the feeling of accomplishment and the views from this unparalleled vantage point.

On a clear day you can see farther than you'd have thought possible. Looking north and a bit east you can see the Sterling Range, Cold Hollow Mountain, Belvidere Mountain, Big Jay, and Jay Peak. If the view is clear, you can see Mount Royal in Montreal just west of north. To the northeast are the Lake Willoughby mountains, Bald and Pisgah.

Swinging east, you can clearly see the Worcester Mountains backed by the Granite Mountains.

South of east is Mount Washington in New Hampshire. The Franconia and Kinsman ranges—also in New Hampshire— extend farther south. The Green Mountains as far as Killington Peak are seen to the south, with Camel's Hump especially prominent. Southwest, you see Whiteface Mountain. Stretching for miles along the western horizon is Lake Champlain and behind it, the Adirondacks.

Follow the white and red blazes south to the Profanity Junction. Taft Lodge is .5 mile along Profanity Trail. Go straight ahead on the Long Trail .2 mile, passing a spur on the right to the Subway (the end of your loop). Soon you will reach the Cliff Trail junction, 1.0 mile from Taft Lodge. To the right is a spur to the other end of the Subway and the Canyon North Extension Trail.

Go left down blue blazed Cliff Trail. The trail drops steeply, and you pass a spur on the right leading a short way to the Cave of the Winds. A huge joint in the bedrock which has closed at the top forms this cave. Be careful to stay back from the edge of the drop-off or you will fall 60 feet into an icy pit!

Continuing on the Cliff Trail, descending over and under rugged boulders, the trail passes a side trail to the Gondola. Go straight ahead through Wall Street, a giant crack with vertical walls. After Wall Street, look sharply as the trail twists and turns abruptly. The trail drops and parallels a ski slope before climbing, and then levels off. You will have many excellent views to the east as you follow the trail through stands of mixed-age spruce and balsam fir.

Steep cliffs rise on your right. The trail follows closely along their base, climbs a narrower ledge, squeezes through a small cave, and ascends abruptly to the right. After reaching level ground you will pass an overlook, and then pass through another crack. Here you climb at a right angle through a narrow cleft. Look carefully for blazes here or you may find yourself on a dead end trail.

Again the trail levels off before beginning a dizzying series of ascents and descents, using ladders in places. Look carefully for sharp twists and climbs. Suddenly you are on level ground, and the Amherst Trail joins from the right. Bear left to the Auto Toll Road, 2.1 miles from Taft Lodge.

Turn right on the road, and follow it across the Long Trail to just behind the large transmission tower. Here, the blue-blazed Canyon Trail goes into the woods on your right. Take the Canyon Trail as it descends steeply, passes through a small cleft, and comes out to the first of many excellent views to the west. Entering the cleft again, you will pass through a narrow opening to the Canyon, a giant rock cleft overhung with slanting rocks. To leave the Canyon, you have the choice of a ladder or a cave—both quite thrilling!

The trail emerges into the woods and soon reaches the junction of the Halfway House Trail. Go straight ahead onto the Canyon North Trail. With little change in elevation, you clamber over and around roots and rocks. There are many fine views to the west, and Sunset Ridge looms ahead. The trail climbs to a cliff base, turns sharply left, and passes through a "windowed" cave. Here you can go three ways (including up and through a cave). Jut follow the blazes to where the three trails merge.

A fork in the trail is soon reached. The path to the right climbs steeply to the Long Trail on the ridge. You will bear left on the Canyon North Extension, and go straight ahead to a spectacular view. You are entering the arctic-alpine zone here, so pass carefully. The going gets rugged again as you pick your way through rock piles and enter another cave.

The trail now climbs and comes out above tree line. Look carefully here for blazes on the rocks, because the trail drops down again. Twisting and turning over huge boulders, it passes under a looming cliff and joins the Subway Trail. The Subway, a giant crack with a roof, can be seen to the right. Rejoin the Long Trail by going five minutes either way on the Subway Trail (both routes are interesting and dramatic).

Back on the Long Trail, go left (north) to the Profanity Junction. Depending on time, weather, or your inclination, descend .5 mile to Taft Lodge, or take a five minute stroll to the Chin. If the day is clear, a sunset from the Chin is unforgettable.

Third Day

Taft Lodge to Butler Lodge, Rock Garden Trail

Class: III
Distance: 4.9 miles
Hiking time: 3.5 hours
Vertical rise: 700 feet

Today is a more leisurely day to wander across the top of the mountain ridge and explore the southern end of Mount Mansfield. Be sure to bring water with you, as Butler Lodge is the next water source.

Hike back up the Long Trail from Taft Lodge .4 mile to Story Trail. This little used trail is one of the most beautiful on Mount Mansfield. Follow it over rocks as it leads you along the west side of the summit, just above tree line. Jagged cliffs rise above you. In .4 mile you reach the Sunset Ridge Trail. Go left here and return in the open to the Long Trail at Profanity Junction.

Go right on the Long Trail and retrace

your steps across the open ledges to the Cliff Trail junction. Continue straight ahead, passing the windswept Lower Lip on your left. You soon dip into the shelter of trees before climbing a short distance to the Upper Lip.

From the Upper Lip, the Long Trail drops and levels off, winding through the many small interconnected colonies of arctic-alpine plants and short, wind-blown conifers. The trail passes to the right of a small alpine bog. This bog is estimated to be over 4,000 years old and it is extremely fragile.

The trail makes its way to Frenchman's Pile, a cairn built where a hiker was killed by lightning many years ago. If a thunderstorm approaches while you are on the mountain ridge, take shelter on one of the many side trails. Hiding in cracks along the ridge offers little protection from the fierce storms that often sweep over Mount Mansfield.

From Frenchman's Pile, the trail descends into trees, crosses the Toll Road, and goes straight ahead to the Summit Station, site of the former Mount Mansfield Summit House. The trail enters the woods again, and passes the west end of the Triangle Trail (tomorrow's route) before reaching the Toll Road again. Follow the road to the left for .2 mile before turning right into the woods. Bear to the right at the junction of the Forehead Bypass, unless the weather is very bad. The trail passes through balsam woods before climbing and crossing two open "bumps" on the Forehead. After dipping into the shelter of trees, the Long Trail reaches the Forehead, whose elevation is 3,940 feet.

The Wampahoofus Trail enters from the right, but you go straight ahead and begin a steep descent. The views to the south here are unsurpassed. Steady downward climbing offers little relief. The trail enters the woods, and a ladder must be negotiated. Continue through the

View to the Lake of the Clouds from Mount Mansfield's Chin

woods and cross to the west side of the ridge. Here the going really gets interesting! Climb down a second ladder, cross a series of ledges which fall off sharply, climb down a third ladder, and the most rugged section of the Long Trail is behind you.

A short distance further brings you to the junction of the Forehead Bypass. Go right and duck through Needles Eye before reaching the junction of the Butler Lodge Trail. Turn right and descend steeply .1 mile to Butler Lodge.

This large log cabin was built in 1933 by the GMC's Long Trail Patrol. The water is in the small brook you crossed just before the lodge. A GMC Caretaker maintains the lodge and the nearby trails.

If the afternoon is young, and you want to stretch your legs, a pleasant jaunt on the Rock Garden Trail is for you. This trail roughly follows the contours for .7 mile to the Maple Ridge Trail, and can be hiked with a day pack round-trip in just over one hour.

The trail starts directly behind Butler Lodge on the Wampahoofus Trail. A short distance from the lodge the trail swings sharply left and climbs a steep rock. At .1 mile, the Rock Garden Trail branches left, and meanders over wooded ledges. Soon the trail enters a large crack in the rocks, and then descends a short way before passing some very large boulders. After a short climb, the trail reaches the Maple Ridge Trail. The views from the open rocks of Maple Ridge (east to Mansfield and west to the Champlain Valley) are breathtaking.

Return to Butler Lodge by the same route.

Fourth Day

Butler Lodge to VT 108 via the Nose

Class: IV
Distance: 4.6 miles
Hiking time: 3 1/2 hours
Vertical rise: 1,250 feet

Today's route takes you over two new areas of interest: The Wampahoofus Trail, and the Nose, Mount Mansfield's second highest point.

Follow the Wampahoofus Trail once again to its junction with the Rock Garden Trail. Continue to the right through fir and spruce woods.

The Wampahoofus Trail leads steeply upward. It twists and turns constantly as it climbs over and around huge boulders. Circling under overhanging ledge, the path becomes wet at times. Step carefully, especially when climbing on wet ledge.

Stands of short, scrawny white birches edge the way as you climb toward massive outcroppings of ledge. The path seems to end abruptly at a high ledge. Climb to the right side and enter the long cave leading upward through the boulders. Overhead a small window through the rocks allows sun to enter the dim interior.

Ahead is an endless variety of rock shapes. Keep a close watch for that petrified creature who roamed the area many years ago. If you have not spotted the elusive Wampahoofus by the time the Maple Ridge Trail intersects at .6 mile, go back about 50 feet and look up. He lies with open jaws, directly overhead to the left.

The Wampahoofus was orignally identified by Professor Roy O. Buchanan, founder of the Long Trail Patrol. According to Roy, the Sidehill Wampahoofus was a creature particularly well adapted to travel on Vermont's mountains. With legs shorter on one side than the other, it was adept at grazing and pursuing prey on the steep slopes. Unfortunately, due to extensive inbreeding all the females were born left-hand runners and all the males right-hand runners. Thus, the males were unable to catch the females during mating season and no more Sidehill Wampahoofuses were born.

From the junction with the Maple Ridge Trail, the Wampahoofus turns sharply right and begins a steep ascent over smooth ledge. Natural indentations in the rock offer convenient footholds here. Scrub trees disappear, as the way continues steeply upward to intersect the Long Trail at the Forehead.

Turn left on the Long Trail and backtrack to the TV Road. Follow the road left and pick up the Long Trail North, which you follow to the base of the Triangle Trail.

The hike up to the Nose on this trail is short and steep. The Nose supports several colonies of almost pure bigelowe sedge so be sure to walk only on the rocks here. The elevation of the Nose is 4,062 feet. Looking back you can see the Lips, Chin, and Adams Apple to the north, and look back down on the Forehead. There are views in all directions.

Blue blazes direct you eastward off of the open rocks. The path leads to a small open lookout on the left. From here you have a spectacular view of the entire eastern side of Mount Mansfield, from the Chin to VT 108.

As you snake over an endless succession of rock, ledge and roots, the footing is slippery and at times precarious. Bushy balsam and spruce surround you.

You soon reach the Toll Road and directly across it is a sign for the Haselton Trail, which will lead you to the base of the mountain. It begins by following the Nose Dive Ski Trail down very steep slopes. You might want to side step a bit, to relieve the pressure on your knees. Go down three turns, and just past the last snow fence on the left (where the Nose Dive goes straight ahead), look to the left for the blue blazes of the Haselton Trail.

The Haselton Trail might aptly be called the "water way." You see, hear, or walk through water almost all the way to the bottom.

The path swings steeply away from the ski trail and passes through wet, rocky areas. It leads over a narrow ski trail, crossing and paralleling trickling brooks in the process. After .5 mile, it traverses a larger ski trail and enters the woods again on the other side.

You cross several smaller brooks before the trail rock-hops over the South Stream. Continuing downward, you suddenly find yourself remaining elevated while streams drop away on both sides.

This hogback becomes soft underfoot as it passes between rows of waist-high evergreens. Needles carpet the path as it proceeds straight and flat along the ridge. Taller firs with needleless limbs are passed before the younger, bushier ones take over again. By this time the streams have become faint rumbles far below.

Returning to its winding ways, the Haselton Trail begins a long, moderate-to-steep descent through thick woods. The path is soft and spongy underfoot. At the 3.4-mile point on this last day's hike it leads out onto a ski service road and follows it down to the Gondola Parking Area.

From here it is a short walk to VT 108 and a little over one mile back to your car.

Additional Information from the Green Mountain Club

The Green Mountain Club welcomes inquiries about hiking and backpacking in Vermont, and about trail conditions and planning. For more information, or to order the Club publications and slide shows described below, write or call:

The Green Mountain Club, Inc.
P.O. Box 889
Montpelier, VT 05602
(802) 223-3463

Guide Books:

Guide Book of the Long Trail — (23rd edition, 1985) Pocket-sized guide with 16 color topographical maps. Complete description of the Long Trail, its side trails and shelters; hiking suggestions and helpful hints.

Day Hiker's Guide to Vermont — (3rd edition, 1987) Companion volume to the *Guide Book of the Long Trail*. Comprehensive coverage of more than 150 short hikes throughout the state, many color and black and white topographical maps, hiking tips and suggestions.

Trail Maps:

Camel's Hump — (1985) Color, fold-out topographical map of the Camel's Hump area; weather resistant, with trail mileages, overnight facilities, trailheads, regulations, and other information.

Mt. Mansfield — (1987) Color, fold-out topographical map of the Mt. Mansfield area; weather resistant, with trail mileages, overnight facilities, trailheads, regulations, and other information.

Mt. Mansfield Booklet:

Tundra Trail — A Self-Guiding Walk: Life, Man and the Ecosystem on Top of Mt. Mansfield, Vermont — This 12-page booklet with illustrations describes a natural history hike along the Long Trail on the summit ridgeline of Mt. Mansfield.

GMC History:

Green Mountain Adventure, Vermont's Long Trail — (1st edition, 1985) An illustrated history of the Green Mountain Club by Jane & Will Curtis and Frank Lieberman. Ninety-six pages of rare black-and-white photographs and anecdotes of the Club's first 75 years.

Pamphlets:

The Long Trail: A Footpath in the Wilderness — Pamphlet with information and suggestions on hiking the Long Trail. Free with self-addressed stamped envelope (SASE).

Day Hiker's Vermont Sampler — Pamphlet with map of Vermont and descriptions of several hikes throughout the state; hiking tips and suggestions. Free with SASE.

Winter Trail Use in the Green Mountains — Pamphlet containing basic information about using the Long Trail system in winter. Free with SASE.

Slide Shows:

Mt. Mansfield — Capstone of Vermont — Color slides and sound narration describes Vermont's highest mountain and its special characteristics, and tells how visitors can help preserve the mountain while they hike it safely. Produced by Louis Borie. 25 minutes.

Beyond the Limit of Trees: New England's Alpine Areas — Color slides and narration provide a close-up look at these unusual natural areas in Vermont, New Hampshire and Maine; with information about their origins and characteristics, the hazards facing them, and the efforts to protect and preserve them. Produced by Peter Zika. 20 minutes.

A fact sheet containing details and rental information for the slide shows is available from the GMC office.

Guidebooks from The Countryman Press and Backcountry Publications

Written for people of all ages and experience, these popular and carefully prepared books feature detailed trail and tour directions, notes on points of interest and natural phenomena, maps and photographs.

Walks and Rambles Series

Walks and Rambles on the Delmarva Peninsula $8.95
Walks and Rambles in Westchester (NY) and Fairfield (CT) Counties $7.95
Walks and Rambles in Rhode Island $8.95

Biking Series

25 Bicycle Tours in New Jersey $8.95
25 Bicycle Tours in Delmarva $8.95
25 Bicycle Tours in Maine $8.95
25 Bicycle Tours in Vermont $7.95
25 Bicycle Tours in New Hampshire $6.95
20 Bicycle Tours in the Finger Lakes $7.95
20 Bicycle Tours in and around New York City $6.95
25 Bicycle Tours in Eastern Pennsylvania $7.95

Canoeing Series

Canoe Camping Vermont and New Hampshire Rivers $6.95
Canoeing Central New York $9.95
Canoeing Massachusetts, Rhode Island and Connecticut $7.95

Hiking Series

50 Hikes in New Jersey $10.95
50 Hikes in the Adirondacks $9.95
50 Hikes in Central New York $8.95
50 Hikes in the Hudson Valley $9.95
50 Hikes in Central Pennsylvania $9.95
50 Hikes in Eastern Pennsylvania $9.95
50 Hikes in Western Pennsylvania $9.95
50 Hikes in Maine $8.95
50 Hikes in the White Mountains $9.95
50 More Hikes in New Hampshire $9.95
50 Hikes in Vermont, 3rd edition $9.95

50 Hikes in Massachusetts $9.95
50 Hikes in Connecticut $8.95
50 Hikes in West Virginia $9.95

Adirondack Series

Discover the Southern Adirondacks $9.95
Discover the South Central Adirondacks $8.95
Discover the Southeastern Adirondacks $8.95
Discover the Central Adirondacks $8.95
Discover the Southwestern Adirondacks $9.95
Discover the Northeastern Adirondacks $9.95
Discover the Eastern Adirondacks $9.95
Discover the West Central Adirondacks $9.95

Ski-Touring Series

25 Ski Tours in Central New York $7.95
25 Ski Tours in Maine $5.95
25 Ski Tours in the Adirondacks $5.95
25 Ski Tours in the White Mountains (revised edition available fall 1988)
25 Ski Tours in Vermont (revised edition available fall 1988)

Other Guides

State Parks and Campgrounds in Northern New York $9.95
The Complete Boating Guide to the Connecticut River $9.95
The Other Massachusetts: An Explorer's Guide $12.95
Maine: An Explorer's Guide $13.95
Vermont: An Explorer's Guide, 3rd edition (spring 1988)
New England's Special Places $10.95
New York's Special Places (spring 1988)

The above titles are available at bookstores and at certain sporting goods stores or may be ordered directly from the publisher. For complete descriptions of these and other guides, write: The Countryman Press, P.O. Box 175, Woodstock, VT 05091.